Exercises in
Interpreting Scripture

Editors:
Lindell Sawyers / Ray T. Woods

JOHN FREDERICK JANSEN

Exercises in
Interpreting Scripture

JOHN KNOX PRESS/Richmond
in cooperation with
THE GENEVA PRESS/Philadelphia

Decade Books Edition

Published by The Geneva Press ® Philadelphia, Pennsylvania

PRINTED IN THE UNITED STATES OF AMERICA

The Covenant Life Curriculum suggests that there are at least three different avenues by which to enter into a study of the Christian faith. You can start with the Bible and see what it says and where it leads you. You can start with the church, God's people, to learn what God has led and is leading them to be and say and do. Or you can start with the daily concerns of life, to see what the Christian faith can tell you about faithful living in the twentieth century. In each case the Bible is basic, the church is involved, and the truth must relate to daily life.

This study is one of three "Bible Studies for Modern Man" for use in 1973 and beyond. Together they offer study materials for an entire year or more, though each can be studied alone. This text, *Exercises in Interpreting Scripture*, provides adults and youth with basic principles of Biblical interpretation and with experience in applying these to four key Biblical passages. *The Covenants in Faith and History*, by Stephen Szikszai, is an overview of the entire Bible through a survey of God's covenants with his people in the Old and New Testaments. *The Word in Action*, by Ross Mackenzie, is a study of the Book of Acts that relates the problems of the early church and the solutions it found to them to the life of our churches today.

The teacher's book, *Leader's Guide to Bible Studies for Modern Man*, gives session-by-session help on leading adults and youth in the study of all three texts.

The denominations that publish these books have produced three other year-long Bible courses for adult-youth study. *The Mighty Acts of God* surveys the entire Bible from Genesis to Revelation in considerable detail (448 pages). *From Bondage to Freedom,* by four different authors, combines in one volume studies of Exodus, Isaiah 40–66, John, and Galatians. The 1970 Bible study resources appeared in three separate and smaller volumes: *Common Sense and the Gospel* (a study of Wisdom literature: Job, Proverbs, etc.); *The Gospel for God's People* (Matthew); and *Living the Gospel* (First Peter). For all of these, detailed teacher's guides are available.

Also part of the Covenant Life Curriculum are three series of studies on the history, doctrine, and life of the church, and three studies on Christian ethics. For further details on any of these, contact any sponsoring denomination: Associate Reformed Presbyterian Church, Cumberland Presbyterian Church, Moravian Church in America, Presbyterian Church in the United States, Reformed Church in America, and (affiliate) The Evangelical Covenant Church of America; or Curriculum Promotion, Box 1176, Richmond, Virginia 23209.

ACKNOWLEDGMENTS

Augsburg Publishing House, for quotations from *For Self-examination*, by Søren Kierkegaard, tr. by Edna and Howard Hong. Copyright 1940 by Augsburg Publishing House.

The Bobbs-Merrill Company, Inc., for a quotation from *The Man Nobody Knows*, by Bruce Barton. Copyright 1924, 1925, 1956 by The Bobbs-Merrill Company, Inc.

Cambridge University Press and Oxford University Press, for quotations from *The New English Bible, New Testament*. © The Delegates of the Oxford University Press and The Syndics of the Cambridge University Press 1961.

Doubleday & Company, Inc., for a quotation from *Genesis* (The Anchor Bible), tr. and with an Introduction and Notes by E. A. Speiser.

Fortress Press, for quotations from *A Thousand Years and a Day: Our Time in the Old Testament*, by Claus Westermann, tr. by Stanley Rudman, copyright 1962 by Fortress Press; *The Significance of the Bible for the Church*, by Anders Nygren, tr. by Carl C. Rasmussen, copyright 1963 by Fortress Press.

Harper & Row, Publishers, Inc., for quotations from *The Bible: A New Translation*, by James Moffatt. Copyrighted 1954 by James Moffatt.

Charles Scribner's Sons, Publishers, for quotations from *A Critical and Exegetical Commentary on Genesis*, by J. Skinner, copyright 1910, by Charles Scribner's Sons, Publishers; *Church Dogmatics*, III/4, by Karl Barth, copyright 1961, copyright by Charles Scribner's Sons, Publishers; *The Parables of the Kingdom*, by C. H. Dodd, copyright 1961, by Charles Scribner's Sons, Publishers.

The Westminster Press, for quotations from *Introducing the New Testament*, by Archibald M. Hunter, published 1958 by The Westminster Press; *A History of Israel*, by John Bright, published by The West-

Contents

Editor's Foreword

THERE IS A *wide variety of books about the Bible designed for use by laymen. This small volume by John Frederick Jansen, however, is unique. It aims not only at being an introduction to the study of the Bible but at being an exercise in Bible interpretation itself. Principles of Biblical interpretation and the practice of interpreting Scripture are both its subjects.*

In Chapter 1, "The Task of the Interpreter," the author outlines some of the pitfalls that await the student of Scripture. After stressing the need for disciplined study of the Bible, he proposes eight questions that should guide the interpreter's inquiry.

In the remaining chapters of the book, Professor Jansen illustrates the task of the interpreter by dealing with four passages from the Bible, two from the Old Testament and two from the New Testament. At least three of the texts chosen for interpretation are notoriously difficult. These passages were chosen for interpretation because they are difficult. But they were also chosen because they raise the kinds of problems that in varying degree are to be found throughout Scripture. Most important, however, these passages deal with meanings that lie at the very heart of the Christian faith. The reader will become involved in questions not only of what the passages meant long ago but of what they mean for the church in today's world. No study of the Bible, however thorough, can deal with all the meanings a passage contains, or resolve all the problems of a given text. Many questions will always remain. The study of the Bible is the work of a lifetime.

The purpose of Decade Books is to provide a brief, introductory treatment of some significant areas of Christian study. The books

11

aim at stimulating further inquiry on the part of the reader. This book, and others in the series, will have served its purpose if it proves to be the starting point for further reflection on the meaning of faith in this generation.

At the end of this book the editors have added a list of aids to the study of the Bible. Many readers may wish to pursue specific problems further by consulting those and other volumes.

Another volume in the Decade series deals with the overall message of the Bible, seen in relation to the giving of the covenant at Mt. Sinai and the inauguration of the New Covenant in Jesus Christ. Its title is The Covenants in Faith and History, *and the author is Stephen Szikszai.* Exercises in Interpreting Scripture *and* The Covenants in Faith and History *are companion volumes.*

Exercises in
Interpreting Scripture

1

The Task of the Interpreter

IN THE eighth chapter of The Acts of the Apostles we are intro-
duced to an Ethiopian official. He is probably a Gentile convert
to Judaism. He has been to Jerusalem to worship and is on his way
home. He is reading from a Bible that he doesn't understand.

We can appreciate his predicament. When we meet for cor-
porate worship we hear the summons, "Hear the Word of God." But
when the Scripture is read, we do not hear it with understanding.
Today there are fresh translations of the Bible and an abundance
of aids for studying it. But for most Christians the Bible remains a
strange book. We are not at home with its Jewishness. Like the ancient traveler, we are strangers to the Book. And we sense, as he
did, that we shall not really be at home in the faith until we are at
home with the Book.

Luke tells us that the Spirit of God prompted Philip to join the
traveler on that desert road. Philip hears the stranger reading aloud
from the fifty-third chapter of Isaiah, that haunting and mysterious
portrayal of the Suffering Servant. Philip asks, " 'Do you understand
what you are reading?' " " 'How can I understand unless someone
will give me the clue?'. . . 'Now,' said the eunuch to Philip, 'tell me,
please, who is it that the prophet is speaking about here: himself
or someone else?' " Then we are told that Philip, beginning with
this passage, "told him the good news of Jesus." (Acts 8: 30-35,
NEB.)

The story suggests that Bible study is not limited to classrooms
or to the times and places of formal worship. It also tells us four
important things about understanding the Bible.

First, the Bible is primarily a confession of faith in a God who has entered human history to claim and to renew mankind. From start to finish, the Bible is a recital in which many voices unite to say, "O come and see what God has done!" This is the way Philip understood it. "Starting from this passage, he told him the good news of Jesus."

Secondly, the Bible speaks of promise and fulfillment. That is why the New Testament cannot be understood apart from the Old. That is why the word once spoken is heard again and again in a new and transforming manner. The Bible is not only the message of God's word and deed but its continuation. The Swedish theologian Anders Nygren has rightly said: "The words of scripture are not addressed only to those to whom they were first spoken. Their meaning is not exhausted by what the prophet and his age saw in them." Philip saw this passage of the Servant fulfilled in Jesus Christ. The apostle Paul would say the same: "For all the promises of God find their Yes in him." (II Cor. 1: 20.)

Thirdly, because God continues to speak through the words of Scripture, the full truth of the Bible is found only in commitment. In our story the Ethiopian stranger responded to the good news of Scripture with his own confession of faith. He was baptized into the community of believers. He went on his way rejoicing, a stranger no more.

Finally, the whole story reminds us that ultimately "God is His own Interpreter, and He will make it plain." In our story the initiative and the direction come from the Holy Spirit. The older confessions of the church speak often of the testimony of the Holy Spirit. For example, the Westminster Confession of Faith says: "Nevertheless we acknowledge the inward illumination of the Spirit of God to be necessary for the saving understanding of such things as are revealed in the Word." Presbyterians have added other confessions, but this reminder is constant. Along with the Confession of 1967 is the question asked of all church officers: "Do you accept the Scriptures of the Old and New Testaments to be the unique and authoritative witness to Jesus Christ in the Church catholic, and by the Holy Spirit God's word to you?"

God is his own interpreter, but the student of Scripture must bring to his task a disciplined mind as well as a warm heart. Faith offers no shortcuts to a responsible reading of the Bible. Nor can we leave the task of Biblical interpretation to a few experts. None of us can avoid the task of interpretation. Every time we listen to someone speak, or whenever we read what someone has written, we interpret what is being said. It is no different when we open the Bible. The question is not whether we need to interpret the Bible, but how well or how badly we do it.

What do we mean by the word "interpret"? The dictionary tells us that "to interpret" means both "to explain" and "to translate." Actually, the two meanings are not far apart. Not many of us are able to translate the Bible from its original languages, but every one of us translates the Bible as he tries to put its message into his own words. Without such translation there can be no explaining of Scripture. For that matter, the New Testament itself uses the same word for explaining and translating. Luke says that the risen Christ met two disciples on the Emmaus road: "And beginning with Moses and all the prophets, he *interpreted* to them in all the scriptures the things concerning himself" (Luke 24: 27). Yet, when the same writer tells us of one "Tabitha, which *means* Dorcas or Gazelle" (Acts 9: 36), he is obviously simply translating a Jewish name for non-Jewish readers. (The Greek verb in both verses is *hermēneuein,* from which we get the word "hermeneutics," or the art of interpretation.)

When we "interpret" a passage of Scripture, we try to find in the passage what is actually there. When we "interpolate," we insert into a passage some material that does not belong there. The scholars who study ancient manuscripts of the Bible remind us that this occasionally happened through the carelessness of a scribe. But each of us has to make sure that he does not do the same thing in his own interpretation. It is very easy to "read into" a passage what is not there.

The word "exegesis" is a technical term for the critical study of a passage of Scripture ("critical" here does not mean finding fault, but refers to a process of careful analysis). Exegesis aims at accurate description of meanings that are actually in the text. The term comes from two Greek words that mean "to lead out." The interpretation of Scripture should deal with meanings that "lead out" from the text rather than with meanings we "read into" the text. In the

New Testament the Greek verb that underlies "exegesis" is used to mean both "to report, to tell" and "to interpret, to explain." In Luke's Easter story, the two returned from Emmaus to Jerusalem and *"told* what had happened [to them] on the road" (Luke 24: 35). But in the Gospel of John the same Greek expression is used in a deeper sense than reporting: "No one has ever seen God; the only Son . . . *has made him known"* (John 1: 18). Just as the same word ("hermeneutics") leads us from translation to interpretation, so the same word ("exegesis") leads us from accurate description to explanation. Both words contain important reminders of the steps involved in understanding Scripture.

What is actually in a text is not always immediately clear. After all, centuries of change separate us from the Biblical writers. Many words that were familiar to their readers are not familiar to us. How can we be true to *their* meaning and still listen for what the Bible has to say to us?

In his book *For Self-examination,* the Danish thinker Søren Kierkegaard imagines a man who has received a letter from his beloved. But this beloved is from another country and the letter is written in a foreign language. (We must not press the illustration by asking how he met her!) The man is naturally eager to read the letter. He sits down with dictionary in hand to translate the prized letter. When a friend happens by and says jovially, "Aha, you are sitting and reading the letter you got from your beloved," the man replies that this is not reading. "If you call that reading, you mock me! No, I am soon finished with the translation, and then—God be praised—then, yes, then I shall read the letter from my beloved. That is something absolutely different."

Of course, the illustration has its shortcomings, for Kierkegaard thinks that this real reading must be done alone. While Biblical understanding is always personal, it should not be cut off from the fellowship of faith where others join us in the study of Scripture. But the illustration does remind us that dealing with the language and history of the Bible is an important first step in receiving its message as a personal address.

Perils and Pitfalls

Interpretation must guard against misinterpretation. What are some of the dangers the interpreter faces?

1. *Assuming too quickly that the Bible says what we think it should say*. We have said that interpretation must "lead out of" a text what is actually there instead of "reading into" a text what we want to be there. Now, every interpreter brings himself to the text. No one of us comes to the Bible without some presuppositions. But we must not assume too quickly that the Biblical writer is asking our questions or shares our viewpoint.

Let us take one example. In the passage from Acts, ch. 8, we read that Philip told the stranger "the good news of Jesus." But who is this Jesus? At the turn of our own century Albert Schweitzer wrote an important book called *The Quest of the Historical Jesus*. He examined all the "Lives of Jesus" written in the nineteenth century and showed how they all were simply the reflections of modern thought. Everyone seemed to find in the Gospels the Jesus he wanted to find.

This temptation is not limited to the professional scholars. In 1924, Bruce Barton wrote a book called *The Man Nobody Knows*. He began with the assumption that Jesus stood for the values of American middle-class, capitalist society. In his preface, Barton said that he had hoped that someday "some one will write a book about Jesus. Every business man will read it and send it to his partners and his salesmen. For it will tell the story of the founder of modern business." And since no one seemed to do it, Barton decided to do it himself. His first chapter is called "The Executive." The motto of his book takes the words of the boy Jesus in Luke 2: 49 in the King James Version: "Wist ye not that I must be about my Father's *business?*"

Contrast this portrait of Jesus with that of Sarah Cleghorn, written in the ferment of revolutionary socialism. The poem is entitled "Comrade Jesus." Part of it runs like this:

"Thanks to Saint Matthew, who had been
At mass-meetings in Palestine,
We know whose side was spoken for
When Comrade Jesus took the floor.

" 'Where sore they toiled and hard they lie,
Among the great unwashed dwell I;—
The tramp, the convict, I am he;
Cold-shoulder him, cold-shoulder me.'

. . . .

"Ah, let no local him refuse!
Comrade Jesus hath paid his dues.
Whatever other be debarred,
Comrade Jesus hath his red card."

These examples point to the need for careful examination of the Gospel records. When we do this it becomes clear that the four Gospels are not "lives of Jesus" in the usual sense at all. They are confessions of faith in One who did not meet the expectations of his own time—or of ours. All four Gospel writers could say with John: "These are written that you may believe that Jesus is the Christ, the Son of God, and that believing you may have life in his name" (John 20: 31).

2. *Hearsay: letting others do our interpreting*. If the first pitfall is the temptation of coming to a passage with our own answers, the opposite pitfall is to assume that we can interpret without any personal involvement. It is the temptation to be content merely to list the opinions of others.

Sometimes we are lured in this direction by going too quickly to the commentaries instead of to the Bible itself. Now certainly, good commentaries are valuable aids for testing and deepening our own insights. But commentaries can stand as a barrier between us and the Biblical passage. At Caesarea Philippi, Jesus asked his disciples not only, "Who do men say that I am?" He went on to ask, "But who do *you* say that I am?" (Mark 8: 27-29).

The Acts of the Apostles contains a story that is both humorous and tragic. Some "fellow travelers" of faith had seen the power of

Paul's ministry in Ephesus. They wanted to use the gospel without becoming disciples themselves. The writer of The Acts says that they "undertook to pronounce the name of the Lord Jesus over those who had evil spirits, saying, 'I adjure you by the Jesus whom Paul preaches.'" But the evil spirit answered, "Jesus I know, and Paul I know; but who are you?" And he left them discomfited. (Acts 19: 13-16.) The same holds true for Biblical interpretation. Hearsay always lacks convincing power.

3. *Long distance: avoiding personal involvement by keeping the Bible in the past.* If hearsay is one way of avoiding personal involvement, another way is to keep the Bible at a safe distance by supposing that it is a book that deals only with the past.

Krister Stendahl reminds us that a Biblical passage must be understood in terms of "what it meant" and "what it means." The interpreter must take both questions into account. To ignore the question of what the passage meant may lead us to read into it what isn't there. But to ignore the question of what the passage means can lead to Bible study that is arid and routine.

So we need to ask "what it meant" with such questions as "Who wrote it? When? To whom? In what circumstances? For what purpose?" This is a necessary filling in of details in which we try to stand at the writer's *point of viewing*. But the question, "What did it mean?" must lead to the question, "What does it mean?" We open the Bible for what it has to say to us now. As a New Testament letter puts it: "For the word of God is living and active, sharper than any two-edged sword, piercing to the division of soul and spirit, of joints and marrow, and discerning the thoughts and intentions of the heart" (Heb. 4: 12).

For that matter, we cannot understand any history without some personal involvement. The historian deceives himself who thinks he can deal with uninterpreted events which can be the raw materials of his study. Historical facts are never "bare" facts. In his book *History Sacred and Profane,* Alan Richardson writes: "There are no uninterpreted facts which form the raw material for the scientific historian; the assumption that there are such facts prevents historians from asking the right questions. *It is not the historian who sticks to the facts; the facts stick to him*" (italics added). We have said that the Biblical writers do not merely report facts but interpret them. How can we hope to understand them if we suppose that we can evade the question of our own involvement in history?

4. *Separating "critical" from "devotional" reading.* We have stressed the importance of both descriptive and personal elements in interpretation. For many Christians, however, a split often occurs between these two. They tend to separate what may be called a "critical" from a "devotional" reading of the Bible.

Now, there are times when we are particularly interested in historical and literary questions, and there are other times, especially in worship, when we listen to the Scripture particularly more as God's personal address to us.

Still, we ought not to isolate "critical" study of the Bible from "devotional" study. If we do so, we may avoid critical questions altogether, or else approach the Bible only as a piece of literature without dealing with it as a testimony of faith. Either course leads to distortion of meaning. We cannot tune out our critical questions when we read the Bible in the setting of worship. Nor can we ignore the claims of the text upon us when we engage in literary and historical study. "What it meant" and "what it means" belong together.

We can make this point from the language of the Bible itself. The language of the Bible is not a heavenly language. It comes out of the doubts and dilemmas of everyday experience. Take the word *doxa,* from which we get the word "doxology." Originally the Greek word meant "opinion." It might be "bewildered opinion." Opinion alongside another opinion is *paradoxa* ("paradox"). The word *doxa* came to mean "good opinion," "reputation." By the time the New Testament was written, however, the secular word *doxa* had already been used to translate the Old Testament word that meant "something solid," "something heavy"—and pointed to the glory of God, "the weight of glory." In Luke's Gospel we can find both meanings brought together in a single sentence. In describing the people's reaction to the wonder of Jesus' healing ministry, Luke writes: "And amazement seized them all, and they *glorified* God ["they gave God *doxa*"] and were filled with awe, saying, 'We have seen *strange things* today'" ("we have seen *paradoxes* today") (Luke 5: 26). This illustration reminds us that if faith is not an escape from life, we should expect the language of the Bible to come out of the language of everyday. Critical study of the Bible can bring to light the source and meaning of Biblical words.

Unfortunately, the phrase "Biblical criticism" still has a negative sound for many people. In some circles "the higher critics" are thought of as the enemies of the Word of God, out to undermine and destroy the foundations of faith. Now, we can admit that *some* Biblical critics past and present have approached the Bible in hostile fashion. Such was Reimarus in the eighteenth century, the man who started the modern "quest of the historical Jesus." He was an impassioned opponent of traditional Christianity. Aside from such hostility, some Biblical critics have been so absorbed in examining the parts of the Biblical writings that they have lost sight of the Bible as a whole. In the words of Davie Napier, some were like medical interns who became "scalpel happy," treating the Bible like a corpse instead of seeing it as a living organism.

But something else needs to be said. The antagonism between critical inquiry and traditional faith was often due to the suspicion with which the church looked upon the work of Biblical scholars. Happily that day is largely past.

In any case, the word "criticism" is not a negative word. Its root meaning comes from the Greek verb *krinein*—a word often used in the New Testament. It means (*a*) to separate, to distinguish, to select, to prefer, (*b*) to consider, to think, to judge, (*c*) to reach a decision, to decide, to pass judgment upon.

"Textual criticism" (formerly called "lower criticism") examines the Biblical manuscripts to decide as nearly as possible what the original probably said. Let us remember that we have no signed originals of Old or New Testament writings. We have thousands of copied manuscripts—and thousands of variant readings. We owe much to textual scholars who have gathered evidence and formed their best judgments as to what the original text probably said. Without their efforts the work of Bible translation could not have been done.

But the same holds true of literary and historical criticism (formerly called "higher criticism"). Such inquiry is equally essential to Biblical interpretation. It seeks to place the Biblical writings in their true historical and literary setting. It studies the influences

that have shaped their form. It examines the relationship of the
Biblical writings to one another and to their times. Such study is an
unending effort to stand as nearly as possible at the Biblical writer's
"point of viewing."

Let us return to Kierkegaard's illustration. Personal encounter
with the Bible as God's Word to us requires a work of "translation."
Critical inquiry will not of itself enable the Bible to speak to us as
the Word of God. Only the interpreting Spirit of God can do this.
But critical inquiry can help to open our ears and our eyes to what
the Word *said* in its own day and prepare us to hear what it *says*
to our day. That is why we ought not to separate "critical" and "devotional" reading of the Bible.

5. *Interpreting words out of context.* To stand at the point of
viewing, the interpreter must guard against reading his own meaning into the words of the Bible. Language, like everything else, is
constantly changing. Take the word "truth." The dictionary will tell
us that the usual meaning of the word is "what is real over against
what is illusory," "what is fact over against what is fiction," etc. But
the dictionary also notes that the word has an "archaic," or older,
usage. In early Anglo-Saxon, the word "trēowth" meant "faithfulness," "troth." The translators of the King James Version intended
precisely this meaning when they translated Ps. 117: 2 as, "The
truth of the LORD endureth for ever." (They took their cue for this
meaning from the Greek translation of the Old Testament.) Since
in modern usage "truth" does not convey the meaning of "troth,"
the Revised Standard Version rightly translates the psalmist's words
as the Hebrew intended it: "The faithfulness of the LORD endures
for ever."

Word study, then, is both necessary and rewarding for our understanding of the Bible. That is why it is wise for the interpreter to
use a concordance and some kind of lexicon or wordbook of the
Bible.

But every method has its dangers. In consulting a concordance
or a wordbook of the Bible, we need to remember that the meaning
of words, in the Bible as anywhere else, must be related to the context in which they appear. When words are divorced from their
setting their study can become highly mechanical and misleading.

After all, a word can have more than one meaning. Consider an example of what happens when this obvious reminder is forgotten. In the *Scofield Reference Bible* (1909), it is assumed that the word "leaven" always carries a negative connotation. After all, "leaven" was to be avoided in the Old Testament Passover ritual (Ex. 12: 15). Jesus spoke unfavorably of "the leaven of the Pharisees and the leaven of Herod" (Mark 8: 15). Paul speaks of "the old leaven, the leaven of malice and evil" (I Cor. 5: 8), and he quotes a proverb of warning that "a little leaven leavens the whole lump" (I Cor. 5: 6; Gal. 5: 9). On that basis, the *Scofield Reference Bible* maintains that Jesus meant something bad when he compared the Kingdom of Heaven to leaven which a woman "took and hid in three measures of meal, till it was all leavened" (Matt. 13: 33; Luke 13: 21). That is then supposed to mean that in its outward forms the Kingdom assumes evil forms! Such word study becomes nonsense. It is not enough to consult a concordance.

The sheer volume of word studies being published today might tempt us to think that particular words have a hidden quality that fixes their meaning forever. But we need to remember that Biblical words, like all words, can be used with great flexibility, depending on the context in which they appear.

6. *Confusing unity with uniformity.* In recent years there has been increased interest in what is called "Biblical theology." We can be grateful for the growing awareness that the varied Biblical writings are all embraced in a unity of faith. That is to say, we can speak of a theology of the Old Testament and not simply of the theologies of an Isaiah or an Amos. And we can speak of a theology of the New Testament and not simply of the theologies of Paul or John. In studying the Bible, we need to consider the whole as well as the parts of Scripture.

But unity is not uniformity. This means that the interpreter has two tasks. On the one hand, he must not impose on the Bible a uniformity that is not there. On the other hand, he must look for a unity of faith that is expressed amid the diversity of expression.

So we must not try to make Paul sound like John, or Isaiah like Hosea. It is a rewarding experience to listen closely to one Biblical voice. We must not allow that voice to be muffled by the others. To use an illustration all too familiar on Sunday morning, the preacher, while shaking hands with Luke, should not already be looking at or talking with Matthew or Mark or John. To be sure, they may have as much or more to tell him. But integrity and courtesy demand that he listen to and speak with the one who is before him. If we mean it when we say in worship, "Hear the Word of God as it is found in . . . ," then we ought to allow that Word to speak to us through the particular passage of Scripture that is read.

Let us illustrate this point another way. In the study of the Gospels, it is very helpful to arrange the four texts in parallel columns to see more clearly what is the same in all of them. But we must resist the temptation to reduce the four Gospels to a "fifth" gospel. If we do that, we will blur the special emphases of each Gospel writer. We can learn a lesson from the second century. Tatian (about the middle of the second century) tried to reduce the four Gospels to a single "harmony" which he called the *Diatesseron* ("From the Four"). For many years the Syrian Church used this *Diatesseron* as its scripture. Ultimately, however, the church rejected this effort to substitute a single gospel for the four Gospels of our New Testament. It may not be an accident that Tatian understood Christianity in a way that the church counted heretical. He was offended by the humanity of Jesus and by the very human way in which the Gospels originated and differed from one another.

What is true of the four Gospels is true of the Bible as a whole. The unity of the Bible is not uniformity. "In many and various ways God spoke of old to our fathers by the prophets," says The Letter to the Hebrews in its opening line—and we could add that "our fathers" responded in quite as many and various ways.

How, then, shall we view the unity of the Bible? Not by trying to make Luke sound like Matthew or John like Paul, but rather, by seeing how each in his own way expresses a central core of Biblical testimony. Says Paul, "I delivered to you as of first importance what I also received." (I Cor. 15: 3.)

Would we have it any other way? Take the apostolic preaching of the cross. Paul says that "Christ died for our sins in accordance with the scriptures"—but there is no one way, and no one Old Testament Scripture, through which the saving deed must be interpreted. Paul appeals to the prophetic word about the "righteousness of God"

which is given us in Christ. He combines imagery of a legal release
with that of a cosmic victory (e.g., Col. 2: 13-15). Luke turns more
to the portrait of the Suffering Servant in Isa., ch. 53, as in our story
of Philip and the stranger. So we could go on. The unity of Biblical
faith is not a drab uniformity. No wonder the church has never been
able to reduce the mystery of the cross to any one doctrine of the
atonement. As one of our hymns puts it:

> "What language shall I borrow
> To thank Thee, dearest Friend,
> For this Thy dying sorrow,
> Thy pity without end?"

Campbell Morgan, an able expositor of a former generation,
wrote: "When I am asked for a theory of the Atonement I ever
reply that in the midst of the mighty movement, the Lord Himself
said 'Why?' and if He asked that question, I dare not imagine that
I can ever explain the deep central verities of His mystery of pain."
(Mark 15: 34.) That is why we need the rich diversity of the Biblical
witness.

SOME QUESTIONS TO GUIDE OUR INQUIRY

Having recognized the pitfalls in interpretation, we can now state
the interpreter's task in a more positive way.

Here are some of the questions that a given text may raise in our
minds. Not every passage raises the same questions, of course, nor
does every question need equal attention. But to varying degrees,
these are the questions that we meet.

1. Does the text raise any problems in translation? Not many
students of the Bible can go to the text of the Hebrew Old Testament or the Greek New Testament to find out firsthand what the
text says. But each reader of the Bible can be aware of particular
problems of translation as they are indicated in the modern editions
such as the Revised Standard Version or the New English Bible.
They are indicated in the margins.

Let us take one example from our story of Philip and the eunuch.
In the King James Version, the passage includes v. 37, which says

that in response to the eunuch's request for baptism, Philip said, "If thou believest with all thine heart, thou mayest," to which the eunuch replied, "I believe that Jesus Christ is the Son of God." The RSV and the NEB put this verse in the margin, so that the text itself moves immediately from v. 36 to v. 38. The margin notes that "other authorities add verse 37." If we look up the passage in a commentary, we soon discover that these "authorities" include some manuscripts belonging to the so-called Western text tradition, and that some of the early church fathers quote this verse. But the verse is not in the great majority of the manuscripts. The verse sounds as if it contained a set of words to be used at baptism. Which came first, the baptismal formula or the text? Did the formula come out of the text of The Acts, or did later worship practices lead to the formula's being inserted into the narrative of The Acts? Since the great majority of the important manuscript witnesses omit the verse, our recent translations are probably correct in omitting the verse. It is easier to explain how it might have been added than it is to explain why it would have been deleted.

In our studies of other passages in the following chapters of this book, we shall meet other questions of translation. A careful reading of the RSV will tell us where and why there are questions of text and translation.

2. What is the form of the text? Is the passage prose or poetry? narrative or sermon? direct or indirect discourse? One of the values of our recent editions of the Bible is that poetry is usually (not always) printed as poetry, and that paragraph divisions help us to recognize the particular units of a writing. The verse numbering, which goes back to 1551, is valuable for reference but does not help us to recognize the units of study.

To recognize poetry as poetry will keep us from reading it as prose. To recognize a parable or a short story will keep us from reading it as literal event. The Book of Jonah is a good illustration of how literary form affects interpretation. How shall we approach this book? It is a prophetic book, but, unlike the other prophetic books, it is largely a story about a prophet rather than a collection of prophetic sayings. Its poetry reminds us of The Psalms. But what of the narrative? Is it history or short story? We should not decide this on the basis of whether *we* believe that the miracle of the fish is possible. We should decide this in terms of what we believe the writer intends. What does he want to convey? When the writer says that the king of Nineveh commanded both men *and cattle* to fast and to don sackcloth and ashes, does that sound like historical narrative or exaggeration for effect, as in a good story?

3. Who wrote it? To be sure, many books of the Bible are anonymous as they stand. Often we do not know the writer by name. Such, for example, is The Letter to the Hebrews, which tradition incorrectly attributed to Paul. All kinds of guesses have been offered as to its authorship. A recent commentary returns to Luther's suggestion that the author is Apollos. But the early church father, Origen, said all that can be stated with certainty: "Who wrote it God knows." Paul did not write it, as John Calvin made quite clear in his day.

So, when we ask, "Who wrote it?" we may or may not be able to identify the writer by name. We can try to find the circumstances in which he wrote and the framework of his thought.

4. To whom is the writer speaking? Who were his first readers? The Biblical writer did not foresee that we would be reading his work today. He wrote for his own generation. If we ask whom the writing is addressed to now, we need to ask to whom it was first addressed. Did the author write to comfort or to condemn? Was he reciting or interpreting a past event or was he describing a situation in his own day? Is his word directed to friends or to foes?

5. When was this Scripture written? Many of the Biblical writings cannot be dated with any certainty. But we can look for the kind of situation that called them forth. Was it a time of peace or of conflict? of prosperity or of distress? of faith or of loss of faith?

Can we find any clues as to the situation described? Do we have access to any other information about the situation, whether from other Biblical writings or from other sources?

Only when we begin to see the kind of situation in which the passage was written are we in a position to ask how that situation compares with ours today. Our situation may not be parallel to that of the writer. We do not need to pretend that we stand where he

stood in order to hear a word for our day. But when we recognize
that God had a compelling word for *that* day, we find it easier to
recognize that God has a word for *our* day. And the word for *today*
comes through the word *then*.

6. What did the writer say? If we are not always certain of the
author's identity or of his exact situation, we can find what he intended to say. Was it to praise or to blame? to comfort or to warn?
to speak a word of promise or of judgment? Is he saying something
new or is he affirming what has already been said?

7. What is the writer's background of thought? Every writing reflects something of the outlook and ways of speaking of its age.
We are people of the twentieth century, and our speech shows it:
"countdown," "cold war," "astronauts," and "smog" are some of the
terms that label us. Similarly, the Biblical writers are people of
their time. This does not detract from the importance of what they
wrote. Rather, it simply means that God speaks and acts in this
world, and he uses human beings as his instruments. When we turn
to the first lines of Genesis, for example, we will not find the outlook of modern astronomy. Why should we? And when we turn to
the Wisdom books such as Job and Proverbs, we will find that they
resemble the wisdom traditions of Egypt and show the influence of
Greek culture. If we look closely at the New Testament, we will
find not only the traditions of the Old Testament but those of the
period between the Testaments as well. In addition, the New Testament shows the influence of Greek and Roman culture. Paul, for
example, quotes pagan literature (I Cor. 15: 33) and makes use of
Stoic style and teaching.

We must be prepared to ask how the Biblical writings reflect their
own time, but we must also ask how they are opposed to it. The
prophet Amos denounces the religious practices and outlook of his
age. And The Book of Jonah is a protest against the narrow national-
ism of its time.

8. How has the text spoken to the community of faith? The words
of the Bible are not static. To understand them we need to go on
a journey with them across the ages. Take the passage from Isa.,

ch. 53, that the Ethiopian stranger was reading. In the Old Testament this passage is one of a number of "Songs of the Servant" that come out of the exile period. The Servant is a puzzling figure. Sometimes the Servant seems to stand for faithful Israel: "Jacob my servant" (Isa. 44: 1); "You are my servant, Israel, in whom I will be glorified" (ch. 49: 3). Sometimes the Servant appears to be an individual who is sent to Israel. His very anonymity makes him stand out in contrast to the actual servant, Israel, as in ch. 42.

Thus we can appreciate the Ethiopian's perplexity. "About whom, pray, does the prophet say this, about himself or about some one else?" We can be sure of one thing. Jewish interpretation did not see the Servant as a messianic figure. He does not seem to be linked with the promised son of David. Yet Philip, as others in the New Testament, found in the Servant a vivid portrait of Jesus the Christ. This does not mean that the prophet of the exile was "predicting" Jesus. Rather, with an insight that was a revelation, he was portraying the kind of servant with whom God was well pleased. That Servant would give himself in total obedience. He would stand for others in selfless love. His suffering would be his credential of glory. The prophet could portray the true Servant—he could not identify him. But Christian faith saw this Servant fulfilled in the life and death of Jesus. Little wonder that Philip, "beginning with this scripture . . . told him the good news of Jesus."

If, within the Bible itself, an old word can be spoken to a new situation, the same holds true in the continuing history of faith. That is why the task of interpretation is never done. When the Pilgrim Fathers left Holland in 1620, John Robinson said in memorable words: "I am verily persuaded that the Lord hath more truth yet to break forth from his holy Word."

THE INTERPRETER AT WORK

In the preceding pages we have dealt in a beginning way with the problems of Biblical interpretation. The purpose of this book, however, is not to be another introduction to Bible study. Many useful introductions are already available. Rather, the remaining chapters of this book will attempt some exercises in Biblical interpretation.

Accordingly, our attention will now turn to four short passages from the Bible. Two are from the Old Testament and two from the New. We shall examine the passages to see the kinds of questions they raise for the interpreter, and we shall suggest clues to finding their meaning. In our efforts at interpretation, we shall be concerned with what the passages *meant* and also what they *mean* for us today. It is our hope that these exercises will sharpen the reader's own skill in Biblical interpretation.

2

Maker of Heaven and Earth

"In the beginning God created the heavens and the earth. The earth was without form and void, and darkness was upon the face of the deep; and the Spirit of God was moving over the face of the waters." (Gen. 1: 1-2.)

IF WE are going to "try our wings" as interpreters of Scripture, we need to place a passage before us and begin to work. But where shall we begin? Why not begin with the opening lines of the Bible itself? "In the beginning God created . . ."

These are familiar words. They are also difficult words. We must not let their familiarity hide this fact.

And we need to see the difficulty for what it is. We need to begin at the right place. Too often we assume that the Biblical account of Creation raised no real questions until the age of modern science. Were that the case, *our* difficulties would lie not in understanding the text but in what we know about the world. But if we begin with the notion that the passage is really out of date, we are not likely to take it very seriously.

To be sure, the modern scientific outlook has raised many new questions for the Christian who wants to take his Bible seriously. It doesn't help our understanding of the Bible when Christians try to block free inquiry through anxious and ill-advised protests. The Scopes trial at Dayton, Tennessee, in 1925, was an example of that. The trial had to do with whether evolution could be taught in the public schools. It did nothing to help the Biblical word about Creation speak forcefully to modern man. On the other hand, it doesn't help to say that the Bible has nothing to do with modern science.

That would suggest that the Word of God and our knowledge of the world have nothing to do with each other.

In any case, if we are to understand the text, we must begin with the text and not with our knowledge of geology or evolution. We will not hear what the text may say to our day unless we first recognize what it said in its own day. Indeed, the greatest difficulty in the text does not lie in the difference between an ancient and modern world view. It lies in our failure to hear what it said and what it says. Our first task is to stand as nearly as we can at the point where the text stands. Before we can judge whether the text's viewpoint can speak to our situation, we need to stand at its "point of viewing." If we use the tools of Biblical study, we can do this to a great extent.

The Text in Its Larger Setting

Before we examine these two verses in detail, we need to see where they occur. Because the Bible begins with the Creation, we might suppose that Old Testament faith began by thinking about creation. This is not so.

After all, the book of Genesis does not stand by itself. It is part of the Pentateuch. These first five books of the Bible are at the very heart of Old Testament faith. Known as the five "books of Moses," they record the history that brought Israel into being. Israel became the people of God through a great event in which God delivered his people from slavery in Egypt. Then he gave them his law at Sinai, led them through the wilderness, and brought them at last into a land of promise.

No one can read the Old Testament without recognizing this great deliverance as the decisive event from Israel's faith in God. It was never told simply as a past event. It was cherished and celebrated over long centuries. We see it reflected in such an ancient "creed" as the one repeated in Israel at the harvest festival:

"And you shall make response before the LORD your God, 'A wandering Aramean was my father; and he went down into Egypt and sojourned there, few in number; and there he became a nation, great, mighty, and populous. And the Egyptians treated us harshly, and afflicted us, and laid upon us hard bondage. Then we cried to the

LORD the God of our fathers, and the LORD heard our voice, and saw our affliction, our toil, and our oppression; and the LORD brought us out of Egypt with a mighty hand and an outstretched arm, with great terror, with signs and wonders; and he brought us into this place and gave us this land, a land flowing with milk and honey. And behold, now I bring the first of the fruit of the ground, which thou, O LORD, hast given me.'" (Deut. 26: 5-10.)

Such a confession of faith reaches back to Israel's earliest years and exposes the heart of Israel's faith. Here nothing is said about the creation of the world. What is said here is that God created Israel by claiming her and making a covenant with her in the midst of her own history.

Little wonder, then, that the opening books of the Bible tell and retell these mighty acts of God in layer upon layer of tradition. For many years Old Testament scholars have recognized at least four major traditions in the Pentateuch. Two of these—called the Yahwist and the Priestly traditions—reach back beyond the exodus to the patriarchal beginnings, to Abraham and to Isaac and to Jacob. But they reach back even farther than that. They begin the story of God's action at the Creation. They do this in order to show that the God who created Israel is the God who created all things.

Let us summarize. When we read the Old Testament as a whole, and Genesis in particular, we soon discover that Old Testament faith rests upon a history of salvation. Israel's faith in God the Creator of heaven and earth did not come before her faith in God the Redeemer. Rather, knowing God as the Creator and the Redeemer of her life, Israel went on to confess that God is the Creator of all. Claus Westermann, in his popular and fascinating book *A Thousand Years and a Day*, says: "Praise of God, the Creator, does not presuppose the creation story, but quite the reverse: praise of God is the source and presupposition of the creation story."

This point is supported in one of the poetic passages from a prophet of the exile:

> "Thus says the LORD, your Redeemer,
> who formed you in the womb:

'I am the LORD, who made all things,
who stretched out the heavens alone,
who spread out the earth . . .' "
(Isa. 44: 24.)

In other words, while Genesis begins with the Creation, its message is anchored to faith in God the Redeemer. Because Israel knew God as her redeemer, she could confess him the Lord of all. It was for this reason that Israel could free her thought about God the Creator from the myths of creation in the ancient world. Her faith was not based on speculation about creation. It was based on an encounter with God in her own history.

THE TEXT IN ITS IMMEDIATE SETTING

The reader of Genesis can readily observe that there are two distinct accounts of Creation (chs. 1: 1 to 2: 4a and ch. 2: 4b-25). A brief comparison of these two will enable us to see more clearly the particular character of the narrative of which our text is part.

The first account portrays the Creation against a background of watery chaos, the second against a background of dry desert. In the first account, water is a threat to creation; in the second it is an assisting element. The first describes the creation of the heavens and the earth by beginning with the heavens; the second is more concerned with the earth in which man is placed. The first account portrays creation in seven majestic days; the second speaks of "the day that the LORD God made the earth and the heavens" (notice that here earth is given primary place rather than heaven). The first account employs the general name for God (*Elohim*) because its tradition held that God's covenant name (*Yahweh*) was not revealed until God said to Moses, "I AM WHO I AM" (Ex. 3: 14). The second account uses the covenant name from the first and links it with *Elohim* (which the RSV translates as "the LORD God"). The first account has the sound of a creed with a pattern of almost liturgical refrains: "and God said," "and it was so," "and there was evening and there was morning," "and God saw that it was good." The second account is much more pictorial and lively. There we read that God formed man from the dust of the ground, breathed into his nostrils, placed him in the garden he had planted, and visited him there. The first narrative describes creation culminating in a sabbath rest. The second sees creation leading quickly into the fall of man. (Genesis, ch. 3, is a continuation of the same narrative.) The first account simply points to man's sexuality: "male and female he created them." The second portrays this sexuality more graphically by describing Adam's (man's) loneliness until Eve is created from his rib to become his other self, "bone of [his] bones and flesh of [his] flesh."

These differences in the two narratives reflect traditions that are widely separated from each other in time and setting. Old Testament scholars agree that the second narrative is the earlier, probably dating from the time of the early monarchy (tenth century B.C.). The first narrative forms the introduction to a Priestly tradition of Israel's beginnings written during or after the time of the exile (sixth century B.C.). For the sake of convenience, scholars label the Priestly tradition P, and the Yahwist tradition J.

Different as the narratives are in form and setting, they are not contradictory but are complementary confessions of faith. Both confess that God is the sole Creator. Both affirm that God has entrusted his world to man. Both insist that man stands in a unique relationship to God. Both begin with the creation of the world in order to chart the purpose of God in calling Abraham and in creating his people. Through both traditions, Israel was able to look back in faith from her own election to the creation of the world and "from there draw the line to herself."

A comparison of the two narratives reminds us that the unity of Biblical faith is not a uniformity; it is a unity that embraces a rich diversity. As Claus Westermann puts it: "Praise of God, the Creator, like his Being, has many voices and forms; it cannot be squeezed into a single type of expression."

The Text Itself: Translation

The Revised Standard Version indicates that the first two verses of Genesis include two problems of translation that will affect our interpretation of their meaning.

We usually read the first verse as a complete sentence: "In the beginning God created the heavens and the earth." In this way, the verse serves as a preface to the whole narrative.

However, the margin of the RSV suggests that another translation is possible. As early as the Middle Ages, some Jewish interpreters insisted that the first verse is not a complete sentence but a relative clause, so that we must go on to read: "In the beginning, *when* God began to create the heavens and the earth, the earth was without form and void, and darkness was upon the face of the deep; and the Spirit of God was moving over the face of the waters."

For that matter, it is possible to take the relative clause into v. 3. In the Anchor Bible volume on Genesis, E. A. Speiser has translated it to read: "When God set about to create heaven and earth— the world being then a formless waste, with darkness over the seas and only an awesome wind sweeping over the water—God said, 'Let there be light.'"

Notice that this question of translation is not a creation of modern criticism. The first alternative was proposed by Ibn Ezra in 1167, the second by Rashi in 1105!

Why the question of translation? Those who read v. 1 as a relative clause (as the RSV margin) do so for reasons of:

Language. Sometimes questions of translation are due to differences in the Biblical manuscripts we have. Here, however, the problem is simply one of grammatical uncertainty. Those who hold that the verse is a relative clause point out that very often the word "in the beginning" (Hebrew: *be reshith*) has the sense of "when." Moreover, the second Creation story also begins with a relative clause: "In the day [meaning "when"] the Lord God made the earth and the heavens . . . ." Grammatically it is possible (and some would say preferable) to read v. 1 as a relative clause.

Theology. When a translation is uncertain, considerations of meaning as well as considerations of grammar influence our decision. To illustrate. Those who read v. 1 as a relative clause make this point: If you read v. 1 as a complete sentence, you raise a problem in v. 2. Is it logical for the writer first to say that God created the heavens and the earth, and then go on to say that the earth was formless and void? Doesn't that suggest that God did a poor job of creating?

The alternative translation of v. 2 gets around this problem by saying that the words about chaos do not follow the statement about creation. They simply provide the setting of creation. That is, God created order out of chaos. If someone should object that this is less than a full and free creation—God only does something with "stuff" that is already there—scholars of this viewpoint have an answer. The Genesis writer, they would say, is not concerned with our questions about a creation *out of nothing*. Such questions came later on. Indeed, not until we come to the Apocrypha, in The Second Book of the Maccabees, written in the first century B.C., do we find a clear expression of a creation out of nothing. There a devout Jewish mother says to her son: "I beseech you, my child, to look at the heaven and the earth and see everything that is in them, and recognize that God did not make them out of things that existed" (II Macc. 7: 28, RSV). In other words, the Priestly writer of Genesis need not have asked this question at all. He used the language of his day—with its portrayal of watery chaos. His only concern was to confess that God created order.

Before we decide, however, let us hear what the defenders of the traditional reading would say in response. After all, the traditional reading still has the support of the RSV translators and a great many commentators. What are their reasons?

Language. Although "in the beginning" might mean "when," the Old Testament does not have enough examples of the word *reshith* to prove that every writer would use the word in the same way. Statistical studies need a larger sampling than is possible here. Moreover, there are some examples where the same word does have a definite time reference, as in Isa. 46: 9-10:

> "I am God, and there is none like me,
>   declaring the end *from the beginning*
>   and from ancient times things not yet done."

This passage does not prove that the traditional reading of Genesis is correct, but it does suggest that it is possible.

History. While we have seen that some interpreters took the alternate reading as far back as the Middle Ages, they were the exception rather than the rule. When the Old Testament was translated into Greek before the time of Christ, the translators understood the text as a complete sentence: "In the beginning God made the heaven and the earth."

Theology. Just as theological considerations of meaning entered the decision for the alternate reading, so they do here. Would not v. 2 pose a bigger problem if we did *not* read v. 1 as a preface? Is not God the lord over chaos? Hard as it may be to conceive of a "created chaos," the prophet of the exile evidently did so:

> "I am the LORD, and there is no other. . . .
> I form light and create darkness,
> I make weal and create woe,
> I am the LORD, who do all these things."
> (Isa. 45: 5, 7.)

A definite statement about creation *out of nothing* is not found until later—but the thought may be there. Since the whole first chapter of Genesis pictures God as the free Creator of all that is, it is hard to believe that the writer would settle for the notion that the chaos came into existence on its own. After all, the whole point of the story is to confess that there is no creation prior to the creating word of God. In the beginning God—and only God.

There is a second question for the translator. The RSV reads "and the Spirit of God was moving over the face of the waters," but the margin reminds us that "wind" can be substituted for "Spirit." Here again, it is not a matter of manuscript differences. In both the Old and the New Testament, the word for "spirit" is also the word for "wind." It is not hard to see how "wind," "breeze," should suggest "breath" and so "spirit." A concordance will show that the choice between "wind" and "spirit" is not easy in a number of passages. For example, the King James Version of Eccl. 1: 17 reads: "I perceived that this also is vexation of spirit," while the RSV reads this verse as: "I perceived that this also is but a striving after wind." In the New Testament we can find a play on words. Jesus says to Nicodemus: "The *wind* blows where it wills, and you hear the sound of it . . . ; so it is with every one who is born of the *Spirit*" (John 3: 8).

Which should it be—wind or Spirit?

Those who read "Spirit" have done so for very different reasons. Christian orthodoxy has seen in this verse a reference to the Holy

Spirit, holding that the same Spirit active in creation is active in the new creation at Pentecost (Acts, ch. 2). We may agree with this theology but we ought not to try to read this theology into the Old Testament text. On the other hand, some read "Spirit" because they see in this verse the imagery of a bird brooding over her nest, suggesting the idea of a world egg that is common in ancient mythology. Traditional Christianity has also been drawn to this image of the brooding Spirit. In the seventeenth century the Puritan poet John Milton began his *Paradise Lost* by invoking the Spirit:

> "Thou from the first
> Wast present, and, with mighty wings outspread,
> Dove-like sat'st brooding on the vast Abyss,
> And mad'st it pregnant . . . ."

However, it is very doubtful whether the text suggests or allows this portrayal. The Hebrew word that means "to brood" or "to move gently" can also mean "to stir up." In Deut. 32: 11, for example, it is used for an eagle and her young. There the imagery is not of brooding but of the mother bird stirring up the nest and fluttering over her young to force them out of the nest. Again, Jeremiah uses the word when he says, "All my bones *shake*" (Jer. 23: 9). In our text the picture of a primeval chaos set over against the power of God hardly suggests a gentle "brooding."

Wind or Spirit? To say "the Spirit of God was moving over the face of the waters" is perfectly all right if we remember that the word "Spirit" here is another way of saying the *power* of God. But then the stress is on God's power over chaos. No wonder that one recent commentator, Gerhard von Rad, prefers the term "storm of God," while another (Speiser) translates "an awesome wind." Speaking of Gen. 1: 2, Alan Richardson writes: "Here the expression is hardly more than a Hebrew idiom meaning 'a very strong wind,' and it can scarcely be used to support a doctrine of the Creator Spirit." (But then Richardson contradicts this statement by turning to the image of God hovering and brooding over the newborn world like a mother bird. The interpreter should not try to have it both ways!)

In this interpretation we choose the image of the strong wind and not that of the brooding bird. The formlessness and the void of chaos are not greater than the strong power of God. Although the word used is not the same, we naturally think of the strong wind that drove back the sea at the exodus (Ex. 14: 21).

So much for the translation itself.

The Text and Its Cultural Background

The first account of Creation has a creedal ring; it is a glowing but restrained confession of faith in God as Creator. Every word has been carefully chosen and finely honed.

Now, before we are ready to ask what this passage may say to us with our world view, we need to ask how it was related to the world view of its own day. We must try to stand with the Biblical writer at his point of viewing. The Priestly writer stood not only within the faith of Israel; he stood also within a particular world of culture. He was a child of his time as well as a child of God.

In saying this, we are showing no disrespect for the uniqueness of Biblical revelation. Quite the contrary. God does not disclose himself in revelation "at long distance." His Word breaks into the actual world where men find themselves.

Modern studies in archaeology and comparative religion have opened up new knowledge of the ancient Near East. From her earliest history, Israel found herself between the cultures of Egypt and Mesopotamia; her own faith and life cannot be isolated from her environment. For a long time, Biblical studies have shown how the legal, ritual, political, and social background of the ancient Near East show through in the way that Israel lived her life and expressed her faith. This should not surprise us. Israel's relationship with Mesopotamia goes back to the earliest days of the Patriarchs.

We shall confine ourselves here to one example of this cultural influence. In 1876, George Smith startled the Christian world by publishing the first fragments of a cuneiform document from an Assyrian library. It is a Mesopotamian epic of creation which has obvious parallels with the Biblical narrative of Creation.

This Babylonian account begins with a description of primeval chaos:

"When in the height heaven was not named,
And the earth beneath did not bear a name,
And the primaeval Apsu, who begat them,
And chaos, Tiamat, the mother of them both,—
Their waters were mingled together . . . ."

In this myth, the powers of chaos, especially the watery monster, Tiamat, determine to destroy the newly generated gods of order. At first Tiamat appears to succeed, but the heavenly powers find a champion in Marduk, the patron god of Babylon. The epic describes a fateful combat in which Marduk conquers Tiamat. We read that he split her up like "a flat fish." With half of the carcass he made a covering for heaven (firmament). With the other half he made the earth. Marduk himself created sun, moon, and stars. Finally, he makes man:

"I will create man, who shall inhabit (the earth),
That the service of the gods may be established."

As the epic closes, the gods assembled to sing the praises of Marduk.

No one doubts that the Babylonian epic is older than the Biblical narrative. Nor can one miss some striking similarities. Both accounts portray a watery, primeval chaos (which the Babylonian account personifies as Tiamat). While the Biblical story has thoroughly taken the mythological element out of the conception of chaos, the Hebrew word *tehom* ("the deep") recalls the Babylonian term. Both accounts see order created out of chaos. But how differently! In the Babylonian myth the gods themselves are generated. In the Biblical narrative God *is*—he is not generated, for he is ever the living God. The Babylonian epic describes creation as a cosmic, touch-and-go struggle. Genesis affirms that creation is the free and sovereign act of God that brooks no resistance. God creates by his word. He speaks—and it is so. In the Babylonian epic, Marduk is himself the god of light. In Genesis, light is God's creation. "Let there be light." The Babylonian epic deifies and personifies the forces of nature that reflect the seasons of the year. Biblical faith knows the Creator as the redeemer, the Lord of history. Finally, the Babylonian epic sees man created out of divine blood. Genesis affirms that although man is created in the "image" and "likeness" of God, he is creature and not divine. (The second Genesis narrative makes this same reminder by portraying man as created from the dust of the ground. Indeed, man's sin lies precisely in his presumption to be "like God.")

The Biblical word undeniably bears the marks of its cultural environment and heritage. Revelation, we repeat, is not at "long distance." Revelation means that God breaks into the world where men find themselves, and is known in and through that history.

"In and through"—but also "over against." Biblical faith finds expression in the speech and thought forms of its time. But Biblical faith is also a new reality. Ancient views of the universe and the gods may explain the manner in which Israel expressed her faith. They do not explain the origin of Israel's faith in God.

Let us take a closer view now of v. 2 of Gen., ch. 1. While dealing above with problems of translation, we asked what the notion of watery chaos might mean. We saw that the Hebrew word *tehom* ("the deep") must have some connection with the Babylonian "Tiamat." By means of this word the ancient world left its trace in the Biblical narrative. But in the Genesis Creation story there is no longer any trace of a mythological monster power who resists God's creative act. We see here a further evidence of the creedal character of this Priestly writing in which every word has been rubbed down to essentials, leaving no room for poetic flights of imagination.

This is not always so in the Old Testament. When the poets describe the Creation, they allow freer rein to the old conception of a struggle against watery chaos. Consider these examples in which the power of chaos is described in more personalized manner:

"Yet God my King is from of old,
    working salvation in the midst of the earth.
Thou didst divide the sea by thy might;
    thou didst break the heads of the dragons on the waters.
Thou didst crush the heads of Leviathan . . . ."

(Ps. 74: 12-14.)

A similar portrayal is found in Ps. 89: 9-10:

"Thou dost rule the raging of the sea;
    when its waves rise, thou stillest them.

> Thou didst crush Rahab like a carcass,
>   thou didst scatter thy enemies with thy mighty arm."

Nor is this freedom confined to the poetry of the Psalter. The prophet cries:

> "Awake, awake, put on strength,
>   O arm of the LORD;
> awake, as in the days of old,
>   the generations of long ago.
> Was it not thou that didst cut Rahab in pieces,
>   that didst pierce the dragon?"
>
> (Isa. 51: 9.)

Prophetic imagination can describe "the days of old" in this way. It can also portray the salvation at the end of time in similar language (e.g., Isa. 27: 1). The same kind of portrayal continues into New Testament times. The book of Revelation, for example, describes the last enemy as a beast who rises from the sea (Rev., ch. 13), while its vision of the end says "and the sea was no more" (Rev. 21: 1).

The poets and prophets knew what they were doing. Their poetic license does not mean a return to mythological belief. But the Priestly recital of Gen., ch. 1, avoids such extravagant imagery altogether. Its sober recital is content simply to say that "in the beginning God"—and God alone!

INTERPRETATION OF GEN. 1: 1-2

1. **"In the beginning."** The first verse of Genesis is a fitting preface to the whole recital which sees the history of Israel as the creation of God and which views Creation itself as a work of God within time. God created "in the beginning"—not in an endlessly recurring cycle that has no beginning or end. Only God is without beginning and without end.

2. **"God."** In Israel, a person's name gives both reality and significance. Among Semitic peoples "El" is a common name for God.

"El" can designate any god. "Elohim" is plural and literally means "gods." However, the striking feature of Old Testament faith is the use of the plural to name the One. It's a way of saying that the whole of the divine is found in the One. The story of creation tells *who* this One is. He is not one or even the chief of many gods. He is the One who is God alone.

3. God "**created**." The verb "to create" (Hebrew: *bara*) in the Old Testament is used only of the divine activity. Even in the Old Testament the word is seldom used, and then chiefly in the Priestly tradition of the Pentateuch and in the later chapters of Isaiah. Perhaps we can see in the use of this word a deepening of Israel's faith during the period of the exile.

God creates. He does not simply fashion and shape what is already there. In the first chapter of Genesis, the verb "to create" is used only in vs. 1, 21, and 27, to summarize the divine activity and to call attention to the creation of living creatures and of man. God creates. He created the heavens and the earth (see also Isa. 65: 17). When the psalmist confesses his sin, he knows that only God can "create in me a clean heart . . . and put a new and right spirit within me" (Ps. 51: 10).

4. "**The heavens and the earth**." The Biblical confession knows that God is the Creator of the heavens and the earth. Heaven and earth belong together. What happens on earth has repercussions in heaven. In the New Testament we read that the "whole creation has been groaning in travail" (Rom. 8: 22) and in hope. This hope looks to a time when every tongue in heaven, on earth, and under the earth will unite to acknowledge Jesus Christ as Lord to the glory of God the Father (Phil. 2: 10-11). Of course, these New Testament affirmations take us beyond the intention of the Priestly writer of Genesis. But we are not going beyond his intention when we understand "the heavens and the earth" to mean that there is no nook and cranny in all creation where God is not Lord. If God created the heavens and the earth, we know that we can never limit his presence either to heaven or to earth. This truth recurs throughout the Old Testament. Read the prayer of Solomon at the dedication of the Temple

(I Kings 8: 23, 27-29), or the words of Ps. 139: 7: "Whither shall I go from thy Spirit?"

5. **"The earth was without form and void, and darkness was upon the face of the deep."** How shall we interpret this verse which appears to speculate behind Creation in a way that the Priestly recital apparently will not allow?

Some older commentators tried to account for this verse by seeing here a reference to some primordial fall of Satan which destroyed God's first Creation. Verse 3 then begins the recital of a new creation out of the chaos which the devil had caused. Now, there are Biblical passages that speak of a Satanic revolt and disturbance in the universe, but *this* narrative does not. Nothing in the text allows us to interpret v. 2 in this manner. To do so would contradict the chapter's repeated insistence that "God saw everything that he had made, and behold, it was very good."

Shall we then say that this verse is a reflection of the ancient imagery of chaos? Yes, but for what purpose? Perhaps the best we can do is to suggest what the German Old Testament scholar, von Rad, says:

"Man has always suspected that behind all creation lies the abyss of formlessness; that all creation is always ready to sink into the abyss of the formless, that the chaos, therefore, signifies the threat to everything created. This suspicion has been a constant temptation for his faith. Faith in creation must stand this test. . . . For the cosmos stands permanently in need of this supporting Creator's will."

We cannot be sure that the Priestly writer had this in mind. We do know that elsewhere the Old Testament speaks of waters that close in over the man of faith, and of the deep that is all about him. (For example, Ps. 42: 7; Jonah 2: 2-3.) But in such moments of crisis, the man of faith remembers that God is lord over the floods.

In any case, we must not forget that the Creation narrative puts v. 1 before v. 2. Chaos is not the ultimate reality, for "the Spirit [wind] of God was moving over the face of the waters." The first and the last word is not chaos but Creator.

The Text Today

Having tried to stand as nearly as we can where the Biblical writer stood, we need to ask what the text might say to us where we stand. Our point of viewing must take seriously not only this text but also the world view flowing from modern science.

To begin, let us review some of the ways in which men of faith have tried to link this text with modern science—ways that do not prove very helpful. We should not forget the devotion and scholarly effort that have gone into trying to harmonize "Genesis and geology." But the following attempts do not offer much help:

1. *The "days of Creation" are really epochs.* Because modern science has made it plain that our world came into being through the processes of thousands of years, some Christians want to read the "days" of Gen., ch. 1, as epochs or ages and not as twenty-four-hour days. After all, they say, does not the New Testament say: "But do not ignore this one fact, beloved, that with the Lord one day is as a thousand years, and a thousand years as one day" (II Peter 3: 8)? Does not the psalmist say that "a thousand years in thy sight are but as yesterday when it is past, or as a watch in the night" (Ps. 90: 4)? Don't we sing:

> "A thousand ages in Thy sight
> Are like an evening gone;
> Short as the watch that ends the night
> Before the rising sun."

However, that does not permit us to read *this* Scripture in such manner. "And there was evening and there was morning, one day." (Gen. 1: 5.) *This* Scripture places the Creation in a framework of seven days which culminate in the Sabbath. To make of his "days" our "ages" is to pretend that the Priestly writer stood where we stand instead of letting him stand in his own place of confession.

2. *The passage intends us to understand days of disclosure rather than days of Creation.* One ingenious attempt to reconcile Genesis with geology suggests that the Biblical narrative does not actually

say that God did the creating in seven days, but rather, that he talked about what he had done in seven days. "And God said"—meaning that he told man (Adam?) of his mighty creative work in a seven-day curriculum.

Quite aside from the fact that we cannot read the text in this manner, such an interpretation defeats its own purpose. Despite its zeal to "defend" the Biblical record, it destroys the very intention of the Biblical witness, for this narrative of Creation sees God's glory precisely in the power of his *word*. God spoke, and it was so.

3. *The millennia of geology can be understood through a catastrophe theory of v. 2.* We have already referred to the attempt to explain the second verse through a "catastrophe theory" about what Satan's fall did to a first Creation. This theory has also been employed to make room for the evidence of geological research within a literal interpretation of the Creation narrative. If it did not help to interpret v. 2, neither does it help to find meeting ground with modern science. It is one more attempt to read modern science into the ancient word.

The trouble with all such attempts—even *if* they could achieve a harmony with modern science—is that they try to take the Biblical word out of its own day. This not only is impossible but is something we ought not to want. If the writer, through some divine illumination, were speaking to *our* world of science, it would mean that God had nothing to say to *his* world. Unless God had a word for that age, how can we believe that this ancient word has something to say to us now?

4. A more tempting solution is to say that *Genesis is about religion and not about science.* This is certainly better than artificial attempts to read modern science into an ancient confession of faith. But it does not satisfy. The man of faith—then or now—cannot keep his knowledge in tidy compartments so that the sacred and secular never meet. He cannot believe one thing in the laboratory and another thing in the sanctuary.

In any case, we have no right to say that the Genesis writer does not have any scientific interest. The ancient world did not separate religion and science as we try to do. Because the Priestly writer took the science of his day seriously, we have to take the science of our day seriously. Claus Westermann states this point well:

"If a description of creation which undoubtedly betrays traces of a scientific approach has been inserted into what is really a hymn of praise in Gen. 1, this is of far-reaching significance for us. Praise of the Creator, if properly understood, need not exclude scientific investigation of the growth of the world; but it can fully support it. A scientific passion for investigating the origin of the world can, if properly appreciated, still be joined with the praise of God, the Creator."

He goes on to say:

"If the Priestly writing could include contemporary insight into the growth of the world in its praise of God, the Creator, then in principle the way is opened for linking the scientific insights of later periods also with the recognition of God as Creator—even if they stand in opposition to the cosmology of the Priestly writing."

Here we must leave the matter. This interpreter is not a scientist and does not pretend that he is. But those who are scientists will agree that in a nuclear age we need to ask afresh what faith in creation has to say to our modern age. In doing this, we should not try to transport the Biblical writer into our day. Nor should we try to transport ourselves back into his day. We should ask, rather, how the Word that shaped his life can shape our life today.

In this task we can take some comfort and encouragement from the diversity of the Biblical witness to creation. As Westermann reminded us earlier, the praise of God the Creator has many voices and forms in the Bible and cannot be squeezed into a single expression. We saw this when we compared the Gen., ch. 1, and Gen., ch. 2, accounts of Creation. We also saw it when we compared certain poetic and prophetic writings. Let's take one more example.

Proverbs, ch. 8, gives us a view of creation that reflects a more "modern" age than that of the Priestly writer. It contains a so-called wisdom tradition shaped by Egyptian culture but even more by the new cosmopolitan Greek culture that followed the conquests of

Alexander the Great. Proverbs does not include a doctrine of creation as a prelude to Israel's redemptive history. In Proverbs, creation itself is made a subject for intellectual inquiry. Wisdom is spoken of as a person, as a "master workman" of God who is his instrument in creating (v. 30). The cultural environment of Proverbs is not that of Gen., ch. 1, as a first reading will quickly show. But faith in the Creator is not tied to any one world view.

Now, if the Old Testament can confess joyously that God is the Creator—and can say this in various ways amid cultural and scientific change—does this not say something to us today? Not every Old Testament witness to God the Creator stands where the Priestly writer of Gen., ch. 1, stands. Yet each in his own way and in his own time can praise God as the Creator.

We hear the word of Gen., ch. 1, in a different cultural environment. But that is far less important than the fact that we hear the word of Gen., ch. 1, in a very different relationship. If the writer of Genesis knew that God the Creator is God the Redeemer, we ought to recognize this much more clearly. For we read the word of Genesis in the light of God's new creation in Christ. When we read "In the beginning," we cannot help recalling "when the time had fully come" (Gal. 4: 4). No wonder that the opening verses of Genesis reappear in a new way as the prologue of the gospel of Jesus Christ:

"In the beginning was the Word, and the Word was with God, and the Word was God. He was in the beginning with God; all things were made through him, and without him was not anything made that was made. In him was life, and the life was the light of men. The light shines in the darkness, and the darkness has not overcome it." (John 1: 1-5.)

3

God Is with Us

"Again the LORD *spoke to Ahaz, 'Ask a sign of the* LORD *your God; let it be deep as Sheol or high as heaven.' But Ahaz said, 'I will not ask, and I will not put the* LORD *to the test.' And he said, 'Hear then, O house of David! Is it too little for you to weary men, that you weary my God also? Therefore the Lord himself will give you a sign. Behold, a young woman shall conceive and bear a son, and shall call his name Immanuel. He shall eat curds and honey when he knows how to refuse the evil and choose the good. For before the child knows how to refuse the evil and choose the good, the land before whose two kings you are in dread will be deserted. The* LORD *will bring upon you and upon your people and upon your father's house such days as have not come since the day that Ephraim departed from Judah—the king of Assyria.' "* (Isa. 7: 10-17.)

SINCE the twelfth century the church has greeted the Advent season with its hymn:

"O come, O come, Emmanuel,   Until the Son of God appear.
  And ransom captive Israel,   Rejoice! Rejoice! Emmanuel
  That mourns in lonely exile here   Shall come to thee, O Israel!"

Every Christmas brings the church and the Christian to the Gospel accounts of the nativity of our Lord. Matthew's account of the virgin birth of Jesus portrays it as the fulfillment of this prophetic promise: "All this took place to fulfil what the Lord had spoken by the prophet: 'Behold, a virgin shall conceive and bear a son, and his name shall be called Emmanuel' (which means, God with us)." (Matt. 1: 22-23.)

However, if the prophetic text has inspired hymnody, it has also ignited controversy. When the Revised Standard Version of the Old Testament was published on September 30, 1952, its translation of this passage raised a storm of protest. That fall, newspapers told of "Bible burnings" in which this page was torn from the Bible and burned in anger directed at a "modern criticism" that was denying the virgin birth of Jesus. True, the American Revised Version of 1901 had indicated in its margin that the word "virgin" could be translated "young woman," but now the Revised Standard Version was printing "young woman" in the text itself.

Sometimes emotions make interpretation more difficult. Why does the Revised Standard Version, which translates "young woman" in Isa. 7: 14, translate "virgin" in Matthew's quotation of the prophetic text? Is Matthew's use of Isaiah legitimate? Was Isaiah predicting the birth of Jesus?

The passage is difficult, but that is no reason for us to abandon our effort at interpretation. Studying this passage leads not only to frustrating difficulties but also to the excitement of new insights. The passage has a special interest because it helps us to recognize the way in which the New Testament writers understood and used the Old Testament.

In any case, no matter how difficult the text may be, it has meant much to the faith and the life of the church—and that is reason enough to prompt our inquiry. If, in the process, some of our preconceived ideas are called into question, so much the better. After all, the Bible has a way of calling our unexamined ideas into question.

Before we can be in a position to evaluate Matthew's use of the Isaiah text, we must come as close as we can to the prophet's own point of viewing. What was going on in the world of Isaiah's time that prompted the words of our text?

THE HISTORICAL SETTING

No word is ever spoken in a vacuum. It is always spoken in a particular time and place. Although it is difficult to identify the exact situation in which many Biblical words were spoken, the occasion of this prophetic word is very clear. That is some encouragement as we begin our task.

The seventh chapter of Isaiah opens with a description of a historical crisis. Further information concerning this crisis is provided in II Kings, ch. 16, and in II Chron., ch. 28. It would be helpful to read all three accounts. With the aid of any standard work on Old Testament history and with a map before us, we can visualize the situation.

The year is 735 B.C. After a period of prosperity, the national and international picture has changed drastically for the Northern Kingdom of Israel and for the Southern Kingdom of Judah. Just as the stable reigns of Israel's Jeroboam II (died 747 B.C.) and Judah's Uzziah (died 742 B.C.) were drawing to their respective ends, the dormant power of Assyria awakened with the rise of its monarch Tiglath-pileser III (745–727 B.C.). The giant empire of Mesopotamia not only awakened but began to reach westward.

Isaiah tells us (ch. 6) that he received his call as a prophet in the year that King Uzziah died. Uzziah was followed by Jotham, whom the Biblical historian calls a good king (II Kings 15: 34). When he died in 735 B.C. the young Ahaz assumed the throne just as the international crisis exploded.

For Assyria was moving westward. What would the small states of Palestine do? Pekah, king of Israel, and Rezin, king of Damascus, with some Philistine allies, formed an alliance to withstand the imminent Assyrian threat. To accomplish their purpose the allies needed the help of Judah (as a look at the map will quickly show). However, Judah decided on a course of independent action and wisely refused to join the coalition. At this point Jotham died and Ahaz came to the throne.

Determined to force Judah's help, Pekah and Rezin invaded Judah from the north while the Philistines and the Edomites harassed her from the west and south. The opening narrative in Isa., ch. 7, tells us that Pekah and Rezin intended to depose young Ahaz and to place on the throne a son of a man named Tabeel. Whether he was from the Davidic line or simply a henchman of the allies we do not know. What is clear is that the young King Ahaz faces a situation

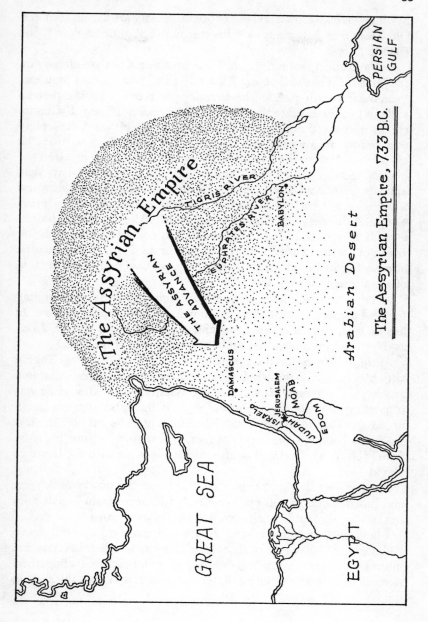

The Assyrian Empire

The Assyrian Empire, 733 B.C.

PERSIAN GULF

TIGRIS RIVER

EUPHRATES RIVER

BABYLON

THE ASSYRIAN ADVANCE

Arabian Desert

DAMASCUS

JERUSALEM

ISRAEL

JUDAH

MOAB

EDOM

GREAT SEA

EGYPT

in which his own crown and the national security are in great danger. Old Testament historians call this the Syro-Ephraimitic War (735–733 B.C.).

As the scene opens in Isa., ch. 7, the invading allies are already on Judean soil. What will young Ahaz do? First, what sort of man was this Ahaz? In our passage he sounds very pious, insisting that he will not put the Lord to the test. But II Kings, ch. 16, and II Chron., ch. 28, tell a different story. There we discover that Ahaz's piety was simply an appeasement of the worst sort. We read that "he even burned his son as an offering" (suggesting that he imitated the human sacrifices of pagan worship). If Isaiah tells us that Ahaz appeals to Assyria for help, the historical records of Kings and Chronicles tell us that he imitated Assyrian worship by securing a copy of the Assyrian altar at Damascus for the Temple in Jerusalem (II Kings 16: 10-16). Ahaz wanted to come to terms with the world of his day. Faced with the danger of invasion, he has decided already to call on Assyria for help. He hopes God will be on the side of the stronger armies.

After all, the situation was serious. Judah's future was hanging in the balance. "When the house of David was told, 'Syria is in league with Ephraim,' his heart and the heart of his people shook as the trees of the forest shake before the wind." (Isa. 7: 2.)

At this juncture God prompted Isaiah to confront the king. Taking with him his son Shearjashub, whose name is a symbol of both doom and hope ("a remnant shall return"), Isaiah met the king as he was inspecting the security of Jerusalem and its water supply. Isaiah urged the king to avoid entangling alliances. The prophetic word is: "Take heed, be quiet, do not fear, and do not let your heart be faint" (ch. 7: 4). God will not forget his covenant with the house of David.

But the king does not trust God. He trusts the power of Assyria and has decided to call on Assyrian help. Once again Isaiah goes to the king, probably at the court. This is where our text begins.

When he first met the king, Isaiah had declared that the Syro-Ephraimitic War would be short-lived. He had warned that Assyrian intervention would lead to the loss of independence altogether. According to our text, the first interview had closed with the ringing

words: "If you will not believe, surely you shall not be established"
(v. 9). Some scholars believed that the text originally might have
read: "The head of Judah is Jerusalem and the head of Jerusalem is
Yahweh" in contrast to the biting way in which the prophet had said
that "the head of Ephraim is Samaria, and the head of Samaria is the
son of Remaliah." Be that as it may, the first interview failed to per-
suade the young king to put his trust in the God of his fathers.

Isaiah knew this. That is why he went back to the king. He dared
Ahaz to "ask a sign of the LORD your God"—so confident was he of
God's promise to Jerusalem.

Notice the phrase "the LORD *your* God." The prophet addressed
Ahaz not merely as an individual but as the representative of the
house of David. The expression recalls the promises that God has
made to the house of David. (See I Kings 1: 17, 36, 47, where the
pronoun "your" underscores the covenant with David's house.)
The implication is that every son of David should trust the Lord his
God. But Ahaz would not do this.

Ask a sign, the prophet challenges the king. Nothing is too great
for God, whether as deep as the grave or as high as heaven. God
can be counted upon! But Ahaz replied, "I will not ask, and I will
not put the LORD to the test."

On the surface, it might seem that the king was more "Biblical"
here than the prophet. Should we seek a sign from the Lord? Do
not Ex. 17: 1-7 and Deut. 6: 16 remind Israel that she must not test
(tempt) the Lord her God? Did not Jesus recall that word of Deu-
teronomy when he was tempted to ask God for a sign (Matt. 4: 7)?
Does not Jesus rebuke his generation for always asking for a sign?

Of course, the New Testament means that Jesus himself is *the*
sign that God has given. To ask for other signs besides "the sign
of the Son of Man" amounts to unbelief. It is one thing to test the
Lord by insisting upon signs or trying to bend God to our bidding.
It is another thing to refuse a sign that God offers. In any case,
Ahaz's pretended piety was a mask for the sign he preferred—
Assyrian help.

Isaiah saw through the pretended piety of the king. "And he said,
'Hear then, O house of David! Is it too little for you to weary men,
that you weary *my* God also?' " Ahaz had chosen not to trust the

Lord his God. So God's man was no longer the king but the prophet who was ready to stake everything on God's promise. "Will you weary *my* God?"

"Therefore." As in Isa. 1: 24; 5: 13, 24; etc., the "therefore" has an ominous character.

Now the sign. We are not yet ready to examine the sign in detail. But the context makes it clear that the child who will be born and will be called Immanuel *will be born very soon*. As the RSV indicates, the translation can read either "a young woman shall conceive" or "is with child." The mother, whoever she is, may or may not already be pregnant. What is the sign? Before this child, soon to be born, can tell good from evil, the crisis of the present will already be over. The child and his name are the sign that God is "with us"— that he has not abandoned or forgotten his covenant with David no matter how faithless the present monarch may be. (For a similar reminder, read Ps. 89: 28-37.)

Our passage from Isa., ch. 7, closes with v. 17, and this verse is rather difficult. On the one hand, it warns of judgment on the house of David similar to that which once had split the kingdom after Solomon's death. Then the northern tribes had seceded with the cry:

"What portion have we in David?
We have no inheritance in the son of Jesse.
To your tents, O Israel!
Look now to your own house, David."
(I Kings 12: 16.)

On the other hand, Isa. 7: 17 points not to civil strife but to the threat of the king of Assyria. Taking the text as it stands, the sign, with its opening and solemn "therefore," closes with a solemn judgment. Four threats follow (vs. 18-25) which amplify the warning of v. 17.

Isaiah 8: 1-4 continues the judgment with another sign, again the sign of a child. This time it is the prophet's own child. For Isaiah has another son and calls his name "Mahershalalhashbaz" ("The spoil speeds, the prey hastes"). The name is an ominous sign of impending judgment. So far we have noticed three signs to Ahaz, each symbolized in a child's prophetic name—"A remnant shall return," "God is with us," and "Spoil speeds, prey hastes." Notice the urgency in these signs. Just as deliverance was pledged before Immanuel would be able to distinguish good and evil, so judgment will overtake an unrepentant king before the young Mahershalalhashbaz can say, "my father" or, "my mother."

The whole section includes a further warning—and a change of imagery. Because the king does not hearken to the sign of a child, Isaiah points to the sign of Shiloah, the small stream that provides Jerusalem with its water supply. The prophet contrasts the "waters of Shiloah" with the great River (the Euphrates, the river of Assyria). Because Judah will not trust the God who provides the waters of Shiloah, God will flood the land with the torrent of Assyrian power. A fearful prospect, indeed! Nevertheless, even this judgment is embraced in a message to the faithful. If the RSV is correct, this last message is actually addressed to Immanuel: "It will overflow and pass on, reaching even to the neck; and its outspread wings will fill the breadth of your land, O Immanuel" (ch. 8: 8).

The prophetic message for this time of crisis includes warning and promise, judgment and salvation. And through it all runs the assurance of God's faithfulness, the promise that he is "with us." Crown and court may take counsel against God, but God's will shall prevail:

> "Take counsel together, but it will come to nought;
> speak a word, but it will not stand,
> for God is with us."   (Isa. 8: 10.)

This section of Isaiah closes by contrasting the way of the people with the way of the prophet. King and people fear Syria and Damascus (recall ch. 7: 2), but the prophet knows that they need only fear the Lord: "Do not fear what they fear, nor be in dread. But the LORD of hosts, him you shall regard as holy; let him be your fear, and let him be your dread" (ch. 8: 12-13). To fear the Lord, however, is to find sanctuary in him. To the man of faith, God is a sanctuary, but to others he will be a stone of offense against which they stumble.

Let us summarize what the context has made clear:

1. The key verse (ch. 7: 14) about the birth of Immanuel cannot be separated from the passage as a whole. Throughout the whole section, "God is with us" is a recurring theme.

2. A particular historical crisis provides the setting of the text, a crisis that threatened national security and the Davidic throne.

3. Isaiah is certain that *this* particular crisis will be short-lived. He is certain that Judah's real crisis lies in her lack of trust in God.

4. The only sign that Ahaz sees or wants is Assyrian power. In contrast, the prophet challenges Ahaz to trust God's sign. But God's ways are not man's ways, and God's sign is given in a little child. (We recall Jesus' words: "I thank thee, Father, Lord of heaven and earth, that thou hast hidden these things from the wise and understanding and revealed them to babes" [Matt. 11: 25].) What a striking contrast! The sign of God is found in the unconscious witness of a child's name—Shearjashub, Immanuel, Mahershalalhashbaz—while the sign that the world sees is Assyria. A later prophet will say to another son of David: "Not by might, nor by power, but by my Spirit, says the LORD of hosts" (Zech. 4: 6).

5. The prophet is not making a prediction about seven centuries later. The sign of Immanuel is a sign for his own time.

THE TEXT IN PARTICULAR: WORDS AND THE WORD

Having seen the sign in its own setting, we can now examine its wording more carefully. The focus of our study now narrows to Isa. 7: 14-16.

1. "Behold, a **young woman** [or, virgin] shall conceive and bear a son."

Is "young woman" or is "virgin" the more accurate to translate the Hebrew of the manuscript text? The word that Isaiah uses is *almah*. However, the specific Hebrew word for "virgin" is *bethulah*. The word *almah* occurs only seven times in the whole Old Testament. It is useful to pause long enough to see what it means in these other places.

Gen. 24: 43-44. "Let the *young woman* who comes out to draw . . .

let her be the woman whom the LORD has appointed for my master's son." This is Rebekah. The King James Version translates "virgin" because v. 16 of this chapter specifically states that she is a *bethulah*, a virgin.

Ex. 2: 8. "So the *girl* went and called the child's mother." The KJV translates "maid." This is Moses' sister. Since she is still at home, we may take it that she is unmarried, young, and doubtless a virgin.

Ps. 68: 25. "The singers in front, the minstrels last, between them *maidens* playing timbrels." The KJV translates "damsels." The festival procession suggests that they are unmarried girls, but this is not expressly said.

Prov. 30: 19. "The way of an eagle in the sky, the way of a serpent on a rock, . . . and the way of a man with a *maiden*." The KJV reads "maid." It is debatable whether this refers to courtship (as we usually take it) or whether it refers to the mystery of procreation, in which case it would not suggest "virgin."

S. of Sol. 1: 3. "Your name is oil poured out; therefore the *maidens* love you." The KJV reads "virgins."

S. of Sol. 6: 8. "There are sixty queens and eighty concubines, and *maidens* without number." The KJV reads "virgins." Evidently, in both instances, the Song of Solomon probably means "virgins."

This list of examples tells us four things: First, the infrequent Old Testament usage of the word *almah* does not allow us to draw definite conclusions from the word itself.

Secondly, although the word is not the specific word for "virgin," it is also not the usual word for "young wife." The word remains vague. In every verse cited above, the word *might* mean "virgin," and in some cases it clearly does mean this. When the Old Testament was translated into Greek, the translators used the Greek word for "virgin," *parthenos,* in Gen. 24: 43 and Isa. 7: 14, while using the word "young woman," *neanis,* in the remaining passages. Thus, Matthew uses "virgin," *parthenos,* because he used the Greek translation of the Old Testament as his source for the quotation.

Thirdly, as the RSV margin indicates, the word in Isa. 7: 14 *might* mean "virgin," because it is not clear whether Isaiah is referring to a damsel who is not yet married ("shall conceive") or whether he means someone who is already "with child."

And fourthly, the text in Isa. 7: 14 does *not* predict the virgin birth of Jesus, for the sign of Immanuel is described as very near. And nothing in the text suggests that the mother will still be a virgin when she has conceived.

In other words, our study reveals that Isaiah's reference to *almah* remains an enigma. The text does not tell us who she is. We do not know whether Isaiah meant someone who was still unmarried or whether he meant someone who was married. Let us remember that we use the word "girl" in the same ambiguous manner, even though technically a "girl" is one who has not yet "put on a woman's name."

One thing is clear. Isaiah's sign is not the "young woman" or "virgin"—but the child and his name. The emphasis is upon Immanuel. Before this child can distinguish good and evil, God will show that he is "with us."

2. "Behold, a young woman [virgin] **shall conceive and bear a son.**" Or should we read: "is with child and shall bear a son"? If the mother is already pregnant, then we should doubtless read "young woman" rather than "virgin." Is Isaiah saying that the Syro-Ephraimitic War will be over in a few months? We cannot be sure. Since the Greek translation of the Old Testament reads "virgin," it naturally puts the conception in the future. There is, however, some reason to read the conception in the present tense. Commentators remind us that in Gen. 16: 11 we have a verse that is nearly identical in form. There the angel of the Lord says to Hagar: "Behold, you are with child, and shall bear a son; you shall call his name Ishmael." The parallel shows that the present tense is perfectly possible and perhaps even probable. If so, the sign is all the more imminent and urgent.

3. "And **shall call** his name Immanuel." Apparently the mother is to name her child. Some commentators have suggested that this gives the mysterious young woman/virgin a greater prominence, holding that the father would normally name the child (see Gen. 5: 3, 29; Isa. 8: 3; Hos. 1: 4; etc.). However, the Old Testament has as many instances where the mother names the child (Gen. 4: 25; 35: 18; Ex. 2: 10; Judg. 13: 24; I Sam. 1: 20; 4: 21; etc.). This does not offer us any clue. Incidentally, the Greek translation reads

"you will call" (referring to Ahaz? possibly suggesting that the child is his son?). Other manuscripts of the Greek translation read "she shall call" or "you [plural] shall call" or "they shall call." Probably the usual reading is the correct one—the mother will name her son Immanuel.

4. "And shall call his name **Immanuel**." The word means "God with us." Many proper names in the Old Testament include the divine name (*J*oshua, *J*ehoiakim, *El*iakim, etc.). Names express faith in God. This does not mean that the person carrying such a name is thought of as divine or semidivine. Nothing in the name, Immanuel, predicts Jesus as the God-Man.

5. "**He shall eat curds and honey** when he knows how to refuse the evil and choose the good." Here the commentators are divided as to the meaning of this description. Some say that "curds and honey" suggest hard times. Since the sign has its ominous and foreboding overtones for Ahaz, "curds and honey" may suggest that deliverance will come only after a time of privation in which the child must share.

Others see in "curds and honey" a sign of hope. The coming deliverance will be for child and people as that time when Israel first came to the "land flowing with milk and honey" (Deut. 6: 3).

Still others point to certain Jewish writings (such as II Enoch 8: 5-6) in which "curds and honey" are the food that the righteous will eat in paradise. If so, the promise is described as a return to the Garden of Eden. Students of comparative religion have linked this with the mythology of the Near East in which "curds and honey" are the food of the gods.

Questions about such details in the text reveal how puzzling the passage remains, and that is all the more reason to take into account the varied interpretations that the text has received. To this we now turn.

THE HISTORY OF INTERPRETATION

What have been some of the principal lines of interpretation of this passage over the centuries?

1. The traditional Christian interpretation reads the Immanuel sign as a clear prediction of Jesus Christ. Naturally, this interpretation is based on Matt. 1: 22-23. Among Christian interpreters this view was not seriously questioned until the eighteenth century. We shall return to this view later when we examine Matthew's use of the text.

2. The interpretation of Isa. 7: 14 as referring to a coming messiah did not begin with the Christian claims about its being fulfilled in Christ. In the closing centuries of Old Testament history, expectation of a messianic king or deliverer became more and more intense. In Isaiah itself passages such as chs. 9: 6-7 and 11: 1-9 are obviously messianic. Those passages proclaim that "a child is born" and "a son is given" who shall receive a mighty name and the throne of David, and on whom the Spirit of the Lord will rest. To be sure, our text does not call Immanuel a son of David, but it is a short road from ch. 7: 14 to those more specific messianic promises. Some scholars have even suggested that Micah, ch. 5, may be an interpretation of Isa. 7: 14. One may question this while yet recognizing some parallel interest. In Micah, ch. 5, one will come forth from Bethlehem "who is to be ruler in Israel." The passage closes with this reminder of the birth of a wonderful child:

> "Therefore he shall give them up until the time
> when she who is in travail has brought forth . . . ."
>
> (Micah 5: 3.)

Since every son of David held messianic promise, it is not surprising that Jewish expositors countered the traditional Christian interpretation in various ways.

In the second century of the Christian era, Aquila undertook a new translation of the Old Testament into Greek, using *neanis* ("young woman") instead of *parthenos* ("virgin"). This allowed a messianic interpretation but not the Christian doctrine of the virgin birth of Jesus.

In the second century the church father Justin Martyr had to meet the criticism of his Jewish opponent Trypho. The latter reminded Justin that *almah* means "young woman." He said that the child must be Hezekiah, the son of Ahaz who succeeded to the throne. Justin replied that the sign would not be a sign unless it spoke of a miraculous birth, but this was scarcely a convincing answer from a Jewish point of view. In the fourth century, however, Jerome met this Jewish interpretation more successfully by showing from II Kings 16: 2 and II Chron. 28: 1 that Hezekiah must already have been born when the sign of Immanuel was given. This led Jewish interpreters to suggest that Isaiah must have referred to some other son of Ahaz whose identity we do not know. (Some recent Jewish interpreters, such as Martin Buber, have returned to the view that the young woman must be the queen and that the child is Hezekiah, pointing out that there are contradictions in the chronologies of Kings and Chronicles.)

3. A nonmessianic interpretation has been suggested by both Jewish and non-Jewish interpreters. This view can take two forms.

Some say that the son is Isaiah's own. Since the text tells us that two of his children bear prophetic names, why not Immanuel also? However, since Isaiah specifically says that Shearjashub and Mahershalalhashbaz are his own sons, why does he not do so with Immanuel? Is it likely that he would call his wife a "young woman" when in Isa. 8: 3 he calls her a "prophetess"?

Others suggest that *almah* can be taken in a generic or collective sense. In this view Isaiah does not refer to any particular woman. He simply says that before any woman can conceive and bear a son God will show his saving presence as "with us."

4. Students of comparative religion suggest that the sign of Immanuel may reflect a mythological idea to be found in the ancient Near East. They read *almah* to mean "virgin," not to find a New Testament fulfillment, but to find reflected here an ancient mythology. For example, in 1929, archaeologists discovered the Ras Shamra tablets which opened up new knowledge about a Phoenician mythology that pervaded Palestine before the Hebrew settlement. To say the least, it is startling to read in these tablets: "Behold a virgin conceive a son." The tablet refers to the goddess Anat. But might Isaiah still make use of a popular pagan belief in a supernatural birth that would be an omen of great good? (Scandinavian scholars

have pointed out that some Jews much later on even thought of
Anat as Yahweh's [the Lord's] consort.) However, when we recall
how constantly Isaiah attacks pagan practices, does it seem likely
that he would make use of such an idea?

There is one school of thought among Old Testament scholars
that holds that Canaanite mythology has left its mark in a cult of
sacred kingship. This cult, they would argue, influenced Israel's
own ideas about kingship. In this cult the king was looked upon as
a "son of God." As such, the king mediated between God and the
people in an annual New Year festival. This festival celebrated the
enthronement of God, and also harked back to the primeval victory
over chaos. (See Chapter 2.) These scholars remind us that Jerusalem was once a Jebusite city with its own traditions. They suggest
that David adopted some of these traditions of "royal ideology"
when he brought the Ark of God into Zion in an enthronement
ritual. (See II Sam., ch. 6.) Now, *if* an ancient mythology of kingship exerted such influence on the worship of God in Jerusalem,
why not suppose that the Immanuel sign reflects something of this
background?

No one questions that the Davidic monarchy brought a new orien-
tation religiously as well as politically into Israel's life. A "theology
of Zion" now joins the "theology of Sinai" to express God's covenant
with his people. And no prophet more clearly affirms a "theology of
Zion" than does Isaiah.

Nonetheless, one may question whether the clue to Old Testament
faith is to be sought in such all-embracing cultural influence. If the
"theology of Zion," like the "theology of Sinai," is grounded in God's
action in history, why speculate further about the influence of
ancient mythology?

5. Reacting against this "myth and ritual" interpretation, other
Old Testament scholars see in the Immanuel sign an attempt to return to an old Israelite conception of the Holy War. We recall how
early Israel carried out her conquest in the conviction that it was
a holy war of God. This view reminds us that in The Book of Judges,
Gideon received a sign from God before he delivered Israel from
the Midianites (Judg. 6: 36-37). Again, in ch. 13: 2-7, the angel of
the Lord announces the coming birth of Samson, who will lead

Israel against the Philistines, in these words: "Behold, . . . you shall conceive and bear a son" (v. 3).

Thus, according to this view, Isaiah demands that Ahaz trust God to do battle again for his people.

The difficulty with this view, however, is that it does not interpret the place of "the house of David."

6. What shall we conclude? While we need not exaggerate the influence of the Near East mythology of kingship, we do need to recognize the influence of a royal cult. Studies in The Psalms have shown that some festival of enthronement seems to be reflected in the "royal psalms." Our reading of Isaiah shows us how central to Isaiah's message are the themes of Jerusalem's throne and Temple. While we have no evidence that Isaiah actually received his prophetic call during an enthronement festival, the enthronement theme is prominent in his call. "In the year that King Uzziah died I saw the Lord. . . . My eyes have seen the King, the LORD of hosts!" (Ch. 6: 1, 5.) Continually the prophet dwells on Jerusalem, aware that the city under judgment is also the holy City of God. (Note the contrast between the picture in ch. 1: 21 f. and that in ch. 2: 2 f. and ch. 4: 2 f.) The prophet addresses "the house of David." He recalls the covenant made with David. One can describe Isaiah's theology as a "theology of Zion."

For light on our passage we turn to some other Old Testament texts that deal with Zion and David. We find these in narrative, in song, and in festival. For example, we may turn to II Sam. 7: 12-16, in which God, through Nathan, addresses David, concluding with the words: "And your house and your kingdom shall be made sure for ever before me; your throne shall be established for ever." Again, in II Sam. 23: 5 (from "the last words of David") we read:

> "Yea, does not my house stand so with God?
> For he has made with me an everlasting covenant,
> ordered in all things and secure."

At Solomon's accession to the throne, Benaiah declared: "Amen! May the LORD, the God of my lord the king, say so. As the LORD has been with my lord the king, even so may he be with Solomon."

(I Kings 1: 36-37.) This covenant which declares that God is with David finds expression not only in the "succession texts" but also in festival songs of enthronement. For example, we find in Ps. 2, a coronation psalm: "He said to me, 'You are my son, today I have begotten you.'" One of the best examples of these royal psalms is Ps. 89, including the lines:

> "I have found David, my servant;
>> with my holy oil I have anointed him;
> so that my hand shall ever abide with him,
>> my arm also shall strengthen him."
>>>>> (Ps. 89: 20-21.)

Other royal psalms are Ps. 72; 132; etc. One of the most familiar "songs of Zion" is Ps. 46, which includes the refrain:

> "The LORD of hosts is *with us;*
>> the God of Jacob is our refuge."

This continual refrain that God is *with Zion* and that he is *with David* is noticeable in Isaiah and especially in the passage that we are studying. After all, "Immanuel" means just that. (See again Isa. 7: 14; 8: 8, 10.) Perhaps the Scandinavian scholar, Ringgren, is correct when he says:

"The young woman may be the queen, the child Immanuel the royal son. The prophet adopts the formula of the official cult, intending to say: 'Take your cultic confession seriously. You say that God is with you; why do you not trust in him? You take the ancient words of the birth of the royal child into your mouths, but you dare not trust the expectations that are bound up with the traditional formula.'" (*The Messiah in the Old Testament.*)

If so, the words need not be specifically messianic, but because they echo the formula of the royal cult, we have the right to read them as messianic—even though no mention is made of a promised son of David.

But does that allow us to identify the queen and the child? No.

As Wilhelm Vischer has put it, a mystery separates this son from all other sons of David. Just as the portrait of the Suffering Servant in Isa., ch. 53, was not a clear prediction of Jesus, but rather, an enigmatic description of the kind of servant who only can accomplish God's will, so here. Neither Hezekiah nor any other son of David who ever sat on the throne of Judah proves to be the promised one. The sign of Immanuel, addressed to a particular crisis long ago, is a sign of hope that in the Old Testament still waits for its fulfillment. Faith rests on hope. As a New Testament letter puts it: "Now faith is the assurance of things hoped for, the conviction of things not seen" (Heb. 11: 1).

God's Word to Israel—and to Us!

We have tried to stand at the prophet's point of viewing. If we have succeeded measurably (we cannot hope to have done so completely) in understanding what the text *meant,* we now must ask what it can *mean* to us. Before we move to the way in which Matthew used the text, we need to ask how we can derive meaning from the text *in its Old Testament setting.*

A few years ago, Walter Cronkite, well-known news commentator, narrated a television series called *You Are There!* The series described a number of historical events, both ancient and modern, that have left their imprint on our Western civilization. Employing the modern means of interview, the series sought to make the audience feel that they "were there." Each program had as its concluding words: "What kind of day was it? A day like all days, filled with those events which alter and illuminate our times—and you are there!" (Incidentally, the series included some Biblical events.)

Insofar as the approach of this television series enabled the audience to stand at the point of viewing, it was both helpful and valid. But insofar as we had to *pretend* that we were there, it was less than satisfying. For we were *not* there. It is neither possible nor necessary to pretend that we were. We live in our day—not in some past day.

Now, Isaiah stood in his age and we stand in ours. He faced a particular national and international crisis that is different from any that we face today. Therefore we must not try to find a point-for-point correspondence between his time and ours, as though Assyria were Russia or China, or Isaiah's counsel about Damascus and Samaria told us what to do about Vietnam or some other trouble spot today. Such an approach would forget the uniqueness of every historical event.

For every historical situation is unrepeatable. To stand at the point of viewing does not mean that we are to forget the distance between Isaiah's day and our own.

Then how are we to approach the text? We can begin by recognizing that God's Word came in judgment and promise where his people were. We can be prepared to hear God do so again. We may try to separate the sacred from the secular, but God does not. He takes secular events seriously—seriously enough to involve himself in them. Whatever else it may be, the Immanuel sign is a genuinely secular sign, for it was addressed to a secular, historical crisis. It challenged Ahaz to trust God not only when he was worshiping in the sanctuary but when he was standing at the crossroads of political decision.

To recognize this will go a long way in helping us to understand why we cannot afford to dismiss the historical events of the Old Testament as though this ancient history is of no concern to us. Why should we be offended, as we sometimes seem to be, by the frank manner in which the Bible describes deplorable events, both national and personal—often in rather grisly detail. Duplicity and deceit, hypocrisy and cowardice, recklessness and callousness—we meet them all (and not least in the narratives of David and his dynasty). But we need these reminders that God does not meet us in some make-believe world but in the rough-and-tumble of *this* world, the world of ambition and greed and power politics and conformity, of illusion and disillusion. Here, where we are, we must be prepared to meet the living God.

And Isaiah understood this. He recognized God's presence and power not only in the worship of the Temple (see Isa., ch. 6) but in the political arena where ch. 7 takes us.

As we look back to the crisis of the eighth century B.C., we can see how Ahaz's refusal to join the coalition enabled Judah to escape the calamity that soon swept the Northern Kingdom away in 721 B.C. But Ahaz's appeal to Assyria signed away Judah's liberty. From now on, Judah would be a vassal state. "Humanly speaking," writes John Bright, "it is difficult, in spite of Isaiah's strictures, to see how Judah could forever have avoided this fate and survived; the day of the independent petty state in western Asia was over. But the consequences of the step were disastrous, as Isaiah said they would be." (*A History of Israel.*)

Isaiah's appeal was neither pious dreaming nor a retreat from political responsibility. It was a challenge to recognize that more than expediency or consensus is needed in the decisions of national and international affairs. Righteousness is needed.

The sign of Immanuel challenged Ahaz to "be quiet" and to "wait." That does not tell us what to do in our day. To try to appropriate those words literally and mechanically might even be betrayal to what God wants us to do today. But the sign of Immanuel does challenge both nation and church not to let expediency or self-interest become the basis for responsible action.

The sign of Immanuel must not become the pretext for doing nothing. We do well to remember, in the turmoil of our day, that a naïve idealism might be as far from genuine faith as is an expedient self-interest. We need to take the dimensions of personal and social sin quite as seriously as Isaiah did. But in *this* time of international tension and nuclear danger, in *this* time of civil unrest and moral uncertainty, the sign of Immanuel can point us to hope and not to despair.

THE OLD WORD BECOMES A NEW WORD

The preceding section has reminded us that we hear Isa. 7: 10-17 in a different situation from that in which the words arose. We face political decisions in the twentieth century and not those of the eighth century B.C.

But our situation is also different in a more basic sense. We come to the Old Testament word of promise as Christians who believe that "all the promises of God find their Yes in him [Christ]. That is why we utter the Amen through him, to the glory of God" (II Cor. 1: 20).

And this is the way Matthew interpreted the text in Isaiah, and the way all the New Testament writers interpreted the Hebrew scriptures. They read them through eyes of faith in the risen Lord.

1. *The Old Testament in the New.* The only Bible that the early church had was the Old Testament. To this Old Testament (especially in its Greek translation) the early church turned to interpret what had happened and what was happening in her midst. For example, when The First Letter of Peter quotes Isa. 40: 8, "The grass withers, and the flower falls, but the word of the Lord abides for ever," it adds immediately, "That word is the good news which was preached to you" (I Peter 1: 24-25). Certain that God had spoken his full and final word in Jesus Christ, the early church turned to the written word of the Old Testament in a radically new manner. Recall the way in which Philip interpreted the Song of the Servant to the Ethiopian stranger in Acts, ch. 8. The New Testament writers do not confine their use of the Old Testament to certain specific messianic passages. Rather, as C. H. Dodd has put it, the whole Old Testament becomes the "sub-structure of New Testament theology."

When did this reinterpretation of the Old Testament begin? Did it begin after Pentecost (Acts, ch. 2)? Did it begin with the apostles? But the most original minds of the early church already reflect this understanding of the Old Testament, they do not initiate it. According to the Gospels, Jesus himself began this reinterpretation of the Old Testament. Luke tells us that Jesus began his ministry by reading from Isa., ch. 61 ("The Spirit of the Lord is upon me . . . to proclaim the acceptable year of the Lord"), and declared, "Today this scripture has been fulfilled in your hearing" (Luke 4: 21). This same Evangelist tells us that the risen Lord continued to do this: "And beginning with Moses and all the prophets, he interpreted to them in all the scriptures the things concerning himself" (Luke 24: 27). As prophets like Jeremiah reinterpreted the meaning of the wilderness journey and the meaning of the Temple, Jesus did so in a much more decisive manner.

When Paul says that "all the promises of God find their Yes" in Christ, he gives the best summary of the way in which the early church went to the Old Testament as the witness to Christ.

2. *Some observations from statistics.* A recently published Greek

New Testament includes an index of 21 pages listing the Old Testament quotations, allusions, and parallels found in the New Testament (not counting the references to the Apocrypha). That list includes references to every Old Testament book except the Song of Solomon, and it finds Old Testament references in nearly every book of the New Testament. The index shows that the books of Psalms and Isaiah have the greatest New Testament use. Since we will be considering Matthew's use of the Old Testament, it is interesting to note that the index suggests that Matthew has about 322 quotations or references to the Old Testament, 43 of which come from The Book of Isaiah. A concordance will show that Matthew often introduces an Old Testament quotation with the phrase "that it might be fulfilled" or "then was fulfilled." (There are at least 13, 4 of which occur in his first two chapters dealing with the birth of Jesus.)

What do such statistics show? They confirm what we have already said. The whole Old Testament is read in a new way because Matthew knows, as does every New Testament writer, that the times have been fulfilled. Matthew does not ask what the prophetic word meant for the prophet's own day. He hears in the Old Testament word what God is saying now, in the time of Christ. Is this a legitimate interpretation? If interpretation is concerned not only with what the text *meant* but with what it *means,* then the answer is yes. For the words of Scripture are addressed not just to those to whom they were first spoken. As Anders Nygren puts it: "Revelation is the action of God, coming to its highest culmination in the fact that he sent Christ into our world and thereby bestowed his righteousness on us. But what is the Bible, then? It is both the message of that action and its continuation."

So then, when we open the Old Testament as Christians under the summons, "Hear the Word of God as it is found in Isa. 7: 10-17," we do so as those who live in A.D. and not in B.C.

With this in mind, let us see how Matthew uses this prophetic text and the Old Testament in general.

3. *The Old Testament in Matthew, chs. 1 and 2.* Suppose we take the first two chapters of Matthew, underlining each Old Testament quotation or allusion that we can find. We will quickly see that

Isa. 7: 14 is only one of many such Old Testament references. It stands to reason that Matthew's use of this text will be similar to his use of other texts.

a. *The genealogy.* Matthew begins with a genealogy of Jesus. A comparison with Luke 3: 23-38 shows that each Evangelist constructs a genealogy that illustrates his particular purpose. Luke works back from Joseph to "Adam, the son of God" to show that Jesus is the Savior who has come for every son of Adam. What does Matthew intend?

First, he carefully arranges the genealogy into three divisions of fourteen generations each. This is obviously a deliberate and rather artificial arrangement. Why? Biblical thought, especially under the influence of the apocalyptic tradition, found symbolic meaning in numbers. Since we have lost the clue to Matthew's symbolism, we can try a guess. If seven is a complete number, and if Matthew is thinking of "weeks of generations" (as Dan. 9: 24 thinks of "weeks of years"), *perhaps* Matthew means that there were two weeks of generations in each of the three periods of sacred history beginning with Abraham. In that case, six weeks of generations brings us now to the *seventh*—to the fullness of times in Christ. This is only a guess. But it is not a guess to assume that Matthew intends some symbolism in the three times fourteen generations.

Secondly, Matthew's genealogy tells us something else. If he selects his names, why does he select some of *these* names? We would hide the skeletons in the closet, but Matthew goes out of his way to bring them into the light. Look at the first six verses! It is not simply that Abraham and Isaac and Jacob are far from plaster of Paris saints. Look at the others. "Judah the father of Perez and Zerah *by Tamar*" (what a sordid story of incest is this, Gen., ch. 38). "Salmon the father of Boaz *by Rahab*" (and she is the harlot of Jericho, Josh., ch. 2). "Boaz the father of Obed *by Ruth*" (Ruth is a nice girl but she belonged to a "minority" group, for she was a Moabite). "And David was the father of Solomon *by the wife of Uriah.*" (Couldn't Matthew have put this more delicately? After all, Bathsheba was David's wife by the time of Solomon's birth!) Surely Matthew's intention is clear. Not at some pinnacle of human goodness but in the very history of sin and shame—that is where God has chosen to come to us. What staggering and unbelievable good news is this news of Immanuel—God with us!

b. "You shall *call his name Jesus*, for he will save his people from their sins." (Matt. 1: 21.) The name "Jesus" is the Hebrew name "Joshua" ("Yahweh is salvation"). The first Joshua brought Israel to the Promised Land. The New Testament Joshua brings the Kingdom of Heaven to his people.

c. The sign of *Immanuel* (Matt. 1: 23). Let us leave this quotation from Isa. 7: 14 for the moment and return to it later.

d. "We have seen his *star* in the East." (Matt. 2: 2.) Doubtless Matthew is thinking of Num. 24: 17: "A star shall come forth out of Jacob, and a scepter shall rise out of Israel."

e. "And you, *O Bethlehem. . . .*" (Matt. 2: 6.) Matthew is quoting from Micah 5: 2. We may note that Matthew does not follow the Greek translation of the Old Testament exactly. The phrase "who will govern my people Israel" can be translated literally "he will shepherd my people Israel." This would recall II Sam. 5: 2 and I Chron. 11: 2, in which David is addressed: "You shall be shepherd of my people Israel, and you shall be prince over Israel."

f. "Then, opening their treasures, they offered him *gifts, gold and frankincense* and myrrh." (Matt. 2: 11.) Matthew may be thinking of the royal Psalm 72, vs. 10-11, in which the kings of Sheba and Seba "bring gifts" to the king. More probably he has in mind Isa. 60: 6: "They shall bring gold and frankincense, and shall proclaim the praise of the LORD."

g. The flight to Egypt is described in the words: "This was to fulfil what the Lord had spoken by the prophet, '*Out of Egypt have I called my son*'" (Matt. 2: 15). The quotation in Hos. 11: 1 originally referred only to the first exodus in which God called Israel, his son, out of Egypt. Evidently, Matthew, as other New Testament writers, saw the time of Christ as the new exodus.

h. The slaughter of the innocents is linked with prophecy: "Then was fulfilled what was spoken by the prophet Jeremiah: '*A voice was heard in Ramah, wailing and loud lamentation, Rachel weeping for her children; she refused to be consoled, because they were no more*'" (Matt. 2: 17-18). Jeremiah 31: 15 refers to the exile, recalling Rachel's death at Ramah (Gen. 35: 16-20; I Sam. 10: 2). Rachel had died in giving birth to Benjamin, and Jeremiah transposes her tears into a mourning for those whom the exile had taken, adding that mourning will yet be changed to rejoicing. Matthew uses the prophetic word to describe the lament for the slaughtered infants of Bethlehem. Indeed, he says, history is filled with tears for God's people who must suffer unjustly.

i. *"For those who sought the child's life are dead."* (Matt. 2: 20.) The heavenly message to Joseph recalls Ex. 4: 19, where Moses is told: "For all the men who were seeking your life are dead."

j. *"He shall be called a Nazarene."* (Matt. 2: 23.) Linguists tell us that this word derivation is not accurate. But in pronunciation there is similarity between the Aramaic word for Nazareth and the Hebrew word for "branch" (*netzer*). Perhaps Matthew is thinking of Isa. 11: 1: "There shall come forth a shoot from the stump of Jesse, and a branch shall grow out of his roots."

These are samplings. Matthew's use of the Old Testament in chs. 1 and 2 is not limited to these instances. Because he sees the time of Christ as the new exodus, he portrays the miraculous preservation of the infant Jesus from the hatred of Herod in a manner that recalls the miraculous preservation of the infant Moses from the hatred of Pharaoh. The slaughter of the innocents recalls the attempt of Pharaoh to kill all the male babies of Israel. The death of Herod recalls that Pharaoh died in his attempt to destroy "Israel my son."

4. *Matthew's interpretation of Isa. 7: 14.* We are now ready to turn to Matthew's use of our text. We notice that he introduces Isa. 7: 14 (as Micah 5: 2; Hos. 11: 1; and Jer. 31: 15) with the formula of fulfillment. Clearly he takes over Isa. 7: 14 *in the same way* that he does these other Old Testament scriptures. Since only Micah 5: 2 can be called a specific messianic prediction, we have further confirmation that the early church saw the whole Old Testament as pointing to Jesus Christ.

Matthew's use of the Old Testament is called "typology"—that is, Matthew sees a genuine correspondence between the events of the past and the events of Christ. After all, the same God who spoke in the past has now spoken fully and finally in his Son.

What shall we say, then, about Matthew's use of Isa. 7: 14? Some scholars have suggested that Matthew is not concerned about "the virgin who shall conceive" but only about the child and his name.

This will not do. Matthew has said specifically that Joseph was scandalized by Mary's pregnancy until assured that "that which is conceived in her is of the Holy Spirit." He has said that Joseph "knew her not until she had borne a son." Clearly, Matthew sees the whole text (in its Greek form) fulfilled in the birth of Jesus. He is not asking what the sign of Immanuel may have meant for Isaiah and his time. He declares that *this* is what the text means for the church in the light of the gospel. The old word has become a new word.

"BORN OF THE VIRGIN MARY"

We naturally ask not only whether Matthew's use of the text is legitimate (and we have suggested that from his point of view it is) but what *we* are to think of the doctrine of the virgin birth. The Apostles' Creed confesses that Jesus "was conceived by the Holy Ghost, born of the Virgin Mary . . . ." Is this a necessary and essential part of the Christian faith? Is it true?

What does "true" mean here? Some say that the virgin birth of Jesus is literally true—that the incarnation took place in this way and not in some other. They find no difficulty in believing that the earthly life of Jesus, which closes with the miracle of Easter, should begin with the miracle of Christmas. If the sign of Easter is the empty tomb, the sign of Christmas is the virgin womb.

Other Christians say that the virgin birth is true as poetic imagery and reverent myth are true—as a way of pointing to the glory and greatness of the Savior as the new creation of God.

"No mortal can with Him compare
Among the sons of men."

Here historical and literary considerations are not able to bring us to a decision. Historical and literary criticism can and must examine the way in which Matthew and Luke describe the birth of Jesus. Such examination will ask whether or not the birth story reflects Jewish or non-Jewish influences. But the decision itself, whether *we* believe that Jesus was born of a virgin, is ultimately a theological decision. As such it lies beyond the scope of our present study. For ultimately, the doctrine of the virgin birth of Jesus must be understood, not through Isa. 7: 14, but in terms of New Testament theology and in terms of the history of doctrine.

However, one thing is clear from our study. Only because Christians confessed that Jesus was born of a virgin did they find confirmation in Isa. 7: 14. The doctrine of the virgin birth was not created to fit an Old Testament expectation, for Jewish expectation has never included a belief that the Messiah would be born of a virgin. On this fact J. Gresham Machen, the ablest interpreter of the orthodox view, is in full accord.

What shall we say then? To make the doctrine of the virgin birth a *fundamental* Christian doctrine on which faith in Christ depends forgets that it is *not* a central affirmation in the New Testament. We do not find it as a primary affirmation in the apostolic preaching. Paul, using a formula that is earlier than his letter, simply speaks of "the gospel concerning his Son, who was descended from David according to the flesh and designated Son of God in power according to the Spirit of holiness by his resurrection from the dead, Jesus Christ our Lord" (Rom. 1: 3-4).

On the other hand, to make the virgin birth *expendable* or *peripheral* forgets that those Evangelists who do describe the nativity of Jesus (and do so in a manner clearly independent of one another) both affirm that Jesus was born of the Virgin Mary.

To make the virgin birth an *explanation* or *proof* of the incarnation is to distort its intention. The virgin birth no more proves or explains the sinlessness of Jesus than the empty tomb proves the resurrection. To think that we can prove the sinlessness of Jesus by the manner of his birth would mean that we have to assume the sinlessness of Mary or to suggest that sexual intercourse is the source of sin. Neither has the slightest Biblical warrant. The virgin birth must not and cannot be used to question the full humanity of Jesus.

No, the virgin birth, as the church has understood it, is a sign that points to the miracle of the incarnation. It is a pointer, not a proof. The great miracle, on which everything depends, is the incarnation—that God has come to us in Jesus Christ once and forever. The great miracle of Easter is the resurrection—of which the empty tomb is the sign. The great miracle is Immanuel—God with us, now and forever.

Since the interpreter should be ready to say where he stands, a personal word is in order. This interpreter takes the Christmas gospel—as he does the Easter gospel—at face value. He does not confuse the sign with the mystery to which it points. He rests his faith not on the sign but on the miracle of the incarnation—God with us. He does not forget that the New Testament, and the church today, points to the wonder of God in Christ in a rich variety of expression. But he does not discard or discount *this* sign on that account. He accepts this sign as one divinely given. He therefore can affirm with the historic witness of the church through the centuries: "I believe . . . in Jesus Christ his only Son our Lord; . . . conceived by the Holy Ghost, born of the Virgin Mary . . . ."

THE SIGN WE NEED

But let us return to the prophetic text itself. Once the disciples of Jesus looked at a later Jerusalem and said, "Lord, look at the size of these stones and buildings" only to hear his sobering reminder that not one stone would be left upon another. Our time has seen the collapse of many of the outward supports of Western Christendom. What signs are we ready to trust? Are we distressed that some signs that once seemed so evident are now gone? Once we were more ready to measure the strength of the faith in terms of particular patterns of Sunday observance, etc. Now we live in an age of bewildering and revolutionary change. What signs are left? What sign do we need? It will not be a sign that will enable us to withdraw from the present either into a nostalgic past or into a future. Here where we are is where God confronts us. Here where we are—in an age of social and civil unrest, of international tension, amid the extremes of unparalleled plenty and abject poverty, in an age where the foundations of much that we have held dear are shaking. The sign we need is still the sign that God offers, the sign of Immanuel, God with us. God with us in our perplexity and struggle. God with us in our doubts and dilemmas. God with us in our pain and affliction. But if God be for us, who can be against us? (Rom. 8: 31.)

And he is with us—now and forever. He is with us because "when the time had fully come, God sent forth his Son, born of woman, born under the law, to redeem those who were under the law, so that we might receive adoption as sons" (Gal. 4: 4-5).

Immanuel is more than hoping! Immanuel is a having. The Advent faith of the church declares that he has come and that he will come. And past and future meet in the living present.

> "O come, Thou Day-spring, come and cheer
> Our spirits by Thine advent here;
> Disperse the gloomy clouds of night,
> And death's dark shadows put to flight.
> Rejoice! Rejoice! Emmanuel
> Shall come to thee, O Israel!"

4

The Way of God's Love

"So he told them this parable: 'What man of you, having a hundred sheep, if he has lost one of them, does not leave the ninety-nine in the wilderness, and go after the one which is lost, until he finds it? And when he has found it, he lays it on his shoulders, rejoicing. And when he comes home, he calls together his friends and his neighbors, saying to them, "Rejoice with me, for I have found my sheep which was lost." Just so, I tell you, there will be more joy in heaven over one sinner who repents than over ninety-nine righteous persons who need no repentance.'" (Luke 15: 3-7.)

"What do you think? If a man has a hundred sheep, and one of them has gone astray, does he not leave the ninety-nine on the hills and go in search of the one that went astray? And if he finds it, truly, I say to you, he rejoices over it more than over the ninety-nine that never went astray. So it is not the will of my Father who is in heaven that one of these little ones should perish." (Matt. 18: 12-14.)

According to the first three Gospels, the most frequent and familiar form of Jesus' teaching was the parable. Of these, one of the best known is the parable of the lost sheep, which appears in both Matthew and Luke.

Why select this familiar story in our sampling of the problems of interpretation? Isn't the story clear enough? Here we find no particular problems of translation as we found in the texts that we have considered. The only variant reading in the text which the Revised Standard Version translators thought worth noting is whether Jesus concluded with a reference to "my Father" or to "your Father" (Matt. 18: 14). That does not affect the parable's interpretation. Nor do we find in this parable any difficult theological vocabulary such as we will meet in our study of Rom. 8: 28-30. Why include this parable?

Two reasons prompt this selection. For one thing, the history of parable interpretation shows that the meaning of the parables has been far from self-evident to the church. Indeed, the history of interpretation reveals a bewildering variety of interpretation and misinterpretation. You can verify this variety for yourself. Suppose you and a few of your friends try to reach a conclusion about the meaning of the parable of the unjust steward (Luke 16: 1-9). What a strange story that is!

But the parable of the lost sheep is not such a strange story. Why this parable? One reason is that the parables—and this parable in particular—offer insight into the way the Gospels are written. Because this parable appears in two Gospels in very different settings, we can see that the Gospels are not diaries. Every word and every action of Jesus comes to us through interpretative memory. The Gospel writers do not simply report the words of Jesus. When these Gospels were written the remembered words of Jesus were already part of an ongoing, living tradition. The Evangelists help us to see how the church remembered and used Jesus' words. They do not simply record what Jesus *said;* they address their readers with what Jesus *says* as the living Lord of the church.

The parable before us is a case in point. Matthew and Luke present this parable in very different manner.

WHAT IS A PARABLE?

Unfortunately, the word "parable" has more than one meaning. Literally, the word means a "throwing alongside," a comparison. But the Greek translators of the Old Testament used the word to render a Hebrew word, *mashal,* which has a very wide range of meaning: proverb, taunt, paradox, riddle, "dark" saying, etc. Even in the New Testament the word "parable" can simply mean "proverb." Jesus said, "Doubtless you will quote to me this proverb [the Greek word is "parable"], 'Physician, heal yourself." (Luke 4: 23.) We see that here a concordance is not a sufficient help. Merely looking up the number of times that the word "parable" appears will not help us. For here we are not concerned with proverbs but with parables, the story form that Jesus used.

So we would be wiser to return to the meaning of the word—a comparison. A parable is an extended simile or metaphor, usually in the form of a narrative.

What is a *simile?* When we consult a dictionary we find that a simile is a figure of speech by which one thing or action or relationship is likened to something else, usually with the words "like" or "as." Jesus often used similes. Here is one: "Behold, I send you out *as sheep* in the midst of wolves; so be wise *as serpents* and innocent *as doves*." (Matt. 10: 16.) But when a simile is expanded it easily becomes what we call a parable: "Therefore every scribe who has been trained for the kingdom of heaven is *like a householder* who brings out of his treasure what is new and what is old" (Matt. 13: 51).

What is a *metaphor?* The dictionary defines metaphor as a figure of speech in which a word or phrase that literally means one kind of object or idea is used in place of another, but without making this explicit with "as" or "like." Jesus' teachings are full of metaphors. For example: "Take heed and beware of the *leaven* of the Pharisees and the Sadducees." (Matt. 16: 6.) When a metaphor is expanded it also very easily becomes what we call a parable. An example might be Matt. 12: 43-45.

However, an *allegory* is also the extension of a simile or metaphor. An allegory is a comparison or story that intentionally has a hidden, veiled meaning—usually in every detail. An allegory must be interpreted point by point to be understood. But a parable usually makes a single point and is much more spontaneous and realistic in its description.

Did Jesus use allegory? The parable of the wicked husbandmen (Matt. 21: 33-43) may properly be called an allegory. The vineyard is Israel, the messengers are the prophets, and the son is Christ. What about the parable of the soils in Matt., ch. 13? Did Jesus develop the detailed interpretation which is given there? Or had the early church already developed the story allegorically before the Gospels were written? In any case, we can distinguish a parable from an allegory. An allegory like Bunyan's *The Pilgrim's Progress* is much more contrived than are the parables of Jesus. His parables have a spontaneity and surprise, a lifelike character, that helps us to distinguish them from allegories.

What, then, is a parable? C. H. Dodd gives us a useful description. "At its simplest the parable is a metaphor or simile drawn from nature or common life, arresting the hearer by its vividness or strangeness, and leaving the mind in sufficient doubt about its precise application to tease it into active thought." (*The Parables of the Kingdom.*)

How many parables do we find in the Gospels? (We limit our study to the Synoptic Gospels of Matthew, Mark, and Luke, because although John may have in its background a parable tradition, the parable form is not characteristic of John's Gospel.) How many parables? This depends on our definition—how developed must a simile or metaphor be before we label it as a parable? In his important study *The Parables of Jesus,* Joachim Jeremias does not include the parable of the householder (Matt. 13: 51-52) because he decides that it is more properly called a simile. Yet A. M. Hunter and others include this passage with the parables proper. Accordingly, we must not be surprised if some scholars find as few as thirty parables while others find some sixty or seventy.

Jesus was not the first to use parables, but his parables are in a class by themselves. As A. T. Cadoux puts it: "They stand alone. Nowhere else are there attributed to anyone parables that in number and beauty can be compared with those of the first three gospels." (*The Parables of Jesus: Their Art and Use.*)

Why Did Jesus Teach in Parables?

According to Mark 4: 10-12 (see also Matt. 13: 10-15; Luke 8: 9-10), the disciples asked Jesus why he taught in parables. Jesus' reply is given in these words: "To you has been given the secret of the kingdom of God, but for those outside everything is in parables; so that they may indeed see but not perceive, and may indeed hear but not understand; lest they should turn again, and be forgiven."

What is this supposed to mean? Does Jesus intentionally talk in riddles? Isn't this favoritism? Doesn't he want those who are "outside" to come "inside"?

This notoriously difficult saying has had many different explanations. But we can say four things about it.

First, the last part of the sentence is a direct paraphrase from Isa. 6: 9-10. When the prophet received his call, he was reminded of his people's stubbornness and refusal to listen to the word of God. The words are a sad and somber recognition of men's refusal to hear the word of God. Jesus too has no illusions about human nature and the way in which men will refuse to heed God's word. We need to remember that Mark is the Gospel that stresses most vividly the conflict of Jesus with his contemporaries. It is not surprising, then, that Mark puts this answer of Jesus in its most extreme form.

Secondly, the contrast between "to you has been given" and "those outside" does not mean that Jesus is playing favorites by willfully keeping others away. He means that unless God gives his grace, *no one* can enter into the secret of the Kingdom of God. And this includes the disciples. But God is gracious: "to you has been given." We think of Jesus' words in Matt. 11: 25-27: "I thank thee, Father, . . . that thou hast hidden these things from the wise and understanding and revealed them to babes. . . . And no one knows the Son except the Father, and no one knows the Father except the Son and any one to whom the Son chooses to reveal him." All of the Gospels, and Mark in particular, stress the inability of the disciples to understand. The secret of the Kingdom is not acquired by cleverness or by human effort. The Kingdom is "given."

Thirdly, most students of the Gospels agree that the passage as we have it is more the Evangelist's commentary than it is an actual word of explanation by Jesus himself. It is always hard to know where a word of Jesus ends and where the Gospel's commentary begins. Let us bear in mind that the word "parable" in the Greek Old Testament can also mean a dark, riddlelike saying. Jesus does utter many darkly prophetic words of judgment. Quite possibly, the contrast between "those outside" and "to you has been given" referred originally to Jesus' preaching in general. But Mark, remembering that "parable" could mean a "dark saying," may have taken this to be an explanation for Jesus' use of the parables proper. Matthew does the same. Indeed, in his account Jesus echoes the words of Ps. 78: 2: "I will open my mouth in a parable; I will utter dark sayings from of old."

Fourthly, we must relate this passage to the whole of Jesus' teaching and action. Jesus always went out *to* the multitude. He always made his appeal to "those outside"—not to keep them outside but to invite them inside so that they might enter the Kingdom of God. Nor should we forget that Mark closes this section on parables with a description of the crowds thronging Jesus. "With many such parables he spoke the word to them, *as they were able to hear it.*" (Mark 4: 33.) He taught the crowds. He did not reject them.

We conclude, then, that the direct reference to Isa., ch. 6, as an interpretation of the parables is probably due to Mark's use of "parable" in more than one sense. Yet Mark's interpretation is not beside the point. C. H. Dodd has described a parable as leaving the mind "in sufficient doubt about its precise meaning to tease it into active thought." That puts it psychologically. Mark puts it theologically. Understanding of God's way and will in the world is only possible if God gives this understanding. Without such illumination the whole world remains an enigma in which the footprints of God and the signposts of his Kingdom are present but are not recognized for what they are. That is as true of the parables as it is true of all the words and deeds of Jesus.

Thus, the parables are not merely sermon illustrations. An illustration only makes more clear what is already understood. But the parables confront us with the Kingdom of God, and this Kingdom is only recognized through the eyes of faith. "To you has been given the secret of the kingdom of God."

Interpreting the Parables

If it is true that the Gospel writers sometimes interpreted the parables as "dark sayings," it is certainly true of the way in which the parables were interpreted by the later church. The history of interpretation shows that increasingly men made of the parables involved and intricate puzzles in which each detail had to yield some mysterious meaning.

Let us see what this kind of interpretation has done to the parable of the lost sheep. The shepherd must be Jesus. The ninety-nine who need no repentance become the angels. Augustine, whose allegorical interpretation of the parables often runs wild, found confirmation for this view that the ninety-nine are the angels in Matthew's reminder that the shepherd left them "on the hills." The hills or mountains must be the heights of heaven! But Luke says that the ninety-nine were left in the wilderness! How can a wilderness or desert be heaven? Augustine's teacher, Ambrose, saw no difficulty here. We call "desert" what is abandoned, he said, and when man sinned, he abandoned heaven.

So we could go on. When the shepherd leaves the ninety-nine to seek the lost sheep, it means that Jesus left heaven in the incarnation. The one lost sheep is the human soul of Adam. In an Easter sermon, Gregory of Nazianzus describes the shepherd's search. Finding the sheep, he says, the shepherd puts it on his shoulder "and the wood" (meaning, of course, that Christ bears both the sinner and the cross). When the shepherd returns with the lost sheep we have the bringing together of heaven and earth in the world to come.

Such interpretation is not limited to the early fathers. It was the prevailing pattern well into the nineteenth century. Many of the views expressed above appear in a book by William M. Taylor, *The Parables of Our Savior,* written in 1886. And a very familiar gospel song does it also:

> "There were ninety and nine that safely lay
>   In the shelter of the fold,
> But one was out on the hills away
>   *Far off from the gates of gold.*" (Italics added.)

Now, in spite of such use of allegory, the parable was still able to grip the hearer with its good news of the love of God for the lost. Listen to Jerome in his letter to Theodosius, written in A.D. 374:

"For my part, I am like a sick sheep astray from the flock. Unless the good Shepherd shall place me on his shoulders and carry me back to the fold, my steps will totter, and in the very effort of rising I shall find my feet give way."

After all, does not the Old Testament say that "all we like sheep have gone astray"? Does not the psalmist say that "the Lord is my shepherd"? And does not Jesus say in the Fourth Gospel, "I am the good shepherd who gives his life for the sheep"? It is perhaps not such a far step from such passages to an interpretation of the parable that identifies him with the shepherd. Here again, the gospel song is a good illustration:

> " 'Lord, whence are those blood-drops all the way
> That mark out the mountain's track?'
> 'They were shed for one who had gone astray
> Ere the Shepherd could bring him back.' "

What we need to see, however, is that when we do this the parable is no longer a parable. It has become an allegory of the cross. It may express the gospel of the cross movingly, but it does *not* express the point that Jesus was making in the parable.

As we have indicated, the allegorical interpretation of the parables was a prevailing one until very recent times. The first scholar seriously to challenge this method was Adolph Jülicher. In the 1890's he wrote a very important book on the parables. Jülicher showed how the allegorical method misses the essential character of the parables of Jesus. He held that a parable makes one fundamental comparison and must not be pressed to yield hidden meanings at every point. He reminded the church that the parables were spoken to common people *before* Jesus died and rose again. However, recent study has shown that Jülicher left the work of interpretation only half done. He showed that the parables were not allegories, but he looked in each parable for a general moral truth rather than the specific good news of Jesus' gospel. What happened was that the parables easily became pious platitudes that lost the cutting edge of the gospel.

Recent studies by Dodd and by Jeremias have stressed this point which Jülicher missed—that the parables are not stories with a general message but that they proclaim the particular good news of the Kingdom of God. And these scholars have reminded us that if we are to understand the parables, we must put them back in their own setting.

THE PARABLE IN ITS SETTING

But which setting? "Form criticism" is a method of Gospel study that tries to reconstruct the situations or occasions that produced the Gospel materials. Some form critics hold that we cannot ever hope to recover the life setting of the historical Jesus himself, since everything in the Gospels has been filtered through the resurrection faith of the earliest church. Now, to be sure, the Gospels are confessions of faith and not diaries of what Jesus did and said. Every word and act of Jesus is interpreted inevitably in the light of Easter and in the awareness of the risen Lord's presence. The form critics are quite right when they say that the Gospels do not offer us an objective "quest of the historical Jesus." No. "These are written that you may believe that Jesus is the Christ, the Son of God, and that believing you may have life in his name." (John 20: 31.)

But does this mean that the Gospels have *no* historical concern about Jesus' earthly ministry? Does this mean that the Gospels *only* reflect the time of the early church and not at all the time of Jesus? Did the Evangelists merely collect sayings of Jesus at random without any interest in the life from which they sprang? Is not their good news precisely that Jesus Christ lived and suffered and died and rose once for all? Is not the narrative of his life central to the gospel of his continuing presence as the Lord of Easter?

In this respect our four Gospels differ greatly from such later and noncanonical writings as The Gospel of Thomas. The latter is a collection of 114 sayings, each prefaced with the words, "And Jesus said . . . ." As we shall see, The Gospel of Thomas also includes the parable of the lost sheep, but with a very different interpretation.

We do not need to go as far as some form critics go. If we cannot piece together from our four Gospels a "biography" of Jesus, we do not need to settle for a historical skepticism that ignores the actual life of Jesus. Of course the Gospels reflect the concerns and crises of the early church. But they also point us time and again to the situation of Jesus himself in his encounters with friend and foe.

And here the parable of the lost sheep is a striking example. Matthew and Luke may or may not have had the same written tradition of this parable. Both of them include a story that Jesus himself undoubtedly once told.

We have said that to understand the parables we must place them in their setting. We must now go on to say that every saying of Jesus has a double setting—one in his own life and one in the life of the church that remembered his word.

An allegorical treatment of the parables ignores their life setting. Allegory would blur the differences between Matthew's version of the parable of the lost sheep and that of Luke.

So we return to the question, Which setting? In this particular case, Luke places the parable in the life setting of Jesus. He shows that the parable was occasioned by controversy and conflict. Matthew places the parable in the life setting of the church. The clue to our understanding is found in the audience to which each Evangelist sees this parable addressed. Instead of blurring the difference, we must examine each account separately.

The Parable in Luke

Jesus aroused intense criticism as well as intense devotion. Notice how Luke's chapter begins. "Now the tax collectors and sinners were all drawing near to hear him. And the Pharisees and the scribes murmured, saying, 'This man receives sinners and eats with them.'" (Luke 15: 1-2.)

The religious authorities were scandalized by the company Jesus kept. Tax collectors were despised because they were in the hire of the Roman occupation. They were despised because of their association with Gentiles and their disregard for the Jewish law as well as because of their notorious graft. Who were the "sinners"? Is this simply another name for tax collectors? But by "sinners" are doubtless meant also those who were guilty of other immoral conduct. Luke includes a story of how, while dining with a Pharisee, Jesus was approached by a "woman . . . who was a sinner" (ch. 7: 37). By "sinners," however, we should probably include not only those who led notorious lives but also "the people of the land," the many who did not follow the Pharisees in meticulous observance of the law. To associate with such people was bad enough. To eat with them was positively scandalous. The religious leaders voiced their bitter protest.

So he told *them* this parable. The parable is spoken to his opponents. Jesus does not argue. The parable is his only reply. He vindicates his mission by pointing them to God's love for the lost. In effect, he says, "God loves like that!"

Luke links this parable with two other parables of God's seeking love for the lost. We need not suppose that all three parables originally were spoken together. Even Luke does not say that Jesus told them *these parables*. He says, "He told them *this* parable." Luke, as each of the Evangelists, has no hesitation in grouping together elements in the tradition that serve his purpose. In Luke's chapter, however, the three parables do belong together, for they form a climactic progression—from one sheep in a hundred, to one coin in ten, to one son of two.

What matters is that the parable of the lost sheep is born in controversy. The parable challenges the opponents to see what God is doing in the world, that he is infinitely more concerned about one sinner than a shepherd is concerned over a lost sheep.

In Luke the parable's meaning lies here—and only here. To ask questions about whether the shepherd's leaving the ninety-nine shows a disregard for their safety is quite beside the point. To ask whether there are actually any "righteous who need no repentance" is equally beside the point. The parable points his opponents to God's love for the lost.

The parable does not describe how long or how hard the shepherd must seek before he finds his sheep. The stress is not, as in the gospel song, about "blood-drops all the way" or "many a thorn" or "how deep were the waters crossed." The stress is only on the joy of finding. "Rejoice with me, for I have found my sheep which was lost." Whether Jesus himself concluded the parable with the words, "There will be more joy in heaven over one sinner who repents . . ." or whether this is the Evangelist's commentary, the point is clear. God loves like that! Joachim Jeremias reminds us that "heaven" is a way of referring to God. The joy of heaven is God's own joy.

Accordingly, the Lucan form of the parable, occasioned by controversy, is a spontaneous and joyful vindication by Jesus of his mission. If a shepherd seeks a lost sheep, how much more does God seek the sinner. Jesus does what God is always doing. "It is the 'redemptive joy' of God, of which Jesus speaks, the joy in forgiving." (Jeremias.)

THE PARABLE IN MATTHEW

When we turn to Matthew we are in a very different environment. Matthew's Gospel is characterized by five large blocks in which the teachings of Jesus are collected for the instruction of the church. These are chs. 5: 1 to 7: 29; 9: 35 to 11: 1; 13: 1-58; 18: 1 to 19: 1; 24: 1 to 26: 2. The Revised Standard Version helps us to see that ch. 18 is a section of such collected teaching by its double spacing before and after the chapter.

If Luke writes to vindicate the worldwide scope of the mission of Jesus, Matthew writes more particularly for the gathered church. Of course, Matthew does not forget the worldwide mission, for his Gospel closes with the Great Commission to "make disciples of all nations." But the very structure of this Gospel underscores its character as instruction for the church. Someone has summed up these characteristics of Matthew's Gospel in this jingle:

> "Matthew gives us five discourses,
>   In threes and sevens he likes his sources;
>   He writes to show what O. T. meant
>   With an ecclesiastic bent."

The preceding study has shown us Matthew's use of the Old Testament. His "ecclesiastic bent" can be illustrated from the famous word of Jesus to Peter in ch. 16: 18 that "on this rock I will build my church." (Matthew is the only Evangelist who uses the word "church.") This concern is shown also in the more creedal and liturgical form in which he gives Peter's confession of faith in ch. 16: 16, and in the trinitarian formula of the Great Commission in ch. 28: 19. But his "ecclesiastic bent" is seen most clearly in the way in which he collects and uses the teaching of Jesus for the instruction of the church. And we see this best in ch. 18.

This chapter brings together remembered sayings of Jesus as the church heard and used them for its own life and order. Then, as now, the church was far from a perfect community. Then, as now, the church had to meet pride: "Who is greatest in the kingdom of heaven?" (ch. 18: 1). Then, as now, the church needed to deal in love with the "weaker brother" (I Cor., ch. 8; Rom., ch. 14). "See that you do not despise one of these little ones." (Matt. 18: 10.) The church must learn the mind of Christ when disputes arise: "If your brother sins against you . . ." (ch. 18: 15). Discipline is one of the marks of true community. Church order, whether in the early church or in the church today, may involve discipline, censure, and even excommunication: "If he refuses to listen even to the church, let him be to you as a Gentile and a tax collector" (ch. 18: 17). This is a sobering note. No church can avoid the responsibility of exercising discipline.

But how to exercise discipline in love—there's the rub. The church, as the individual Christian, needs to know what forgiveness means. "How often shall my brother sin against me, and I forgive him?" (Ch. 18: 21.) No wonder that the chapter closes with a parable of forgiveness.

We see that the chapter reflects the regulations which the church must have if it is to be a true community. This chapter is not concerned with the church's mission to the world. Matthew will do that elsewhere. This chapter is addressed to the gathered church. "For where two or three are gathered in my name, there I am in the midst of them." (Ch. 18: 20.)

But let us note that the chapter is more than regulations. It is gospel—good news. That is why Matthew follows the section about the weaker brother and precedes the section about the offending brother with a reminder of what God is always doing, in the church as well as in the world. The solemn responsibility of church discipline is preceded by the parable of the lost sheep. "See that you do not despise one of these little ones!" Then the parable. "What do you think?" (The "you" is addressed to disciples, to the community of faith.) "If a man has a hundred sheep, and one of them has gone astray, does he not leave the ninety-nine in the hills and go in search of the one that went astray?"

What has happened to the parable? Clearly, a parable that in its original setting was a parable of controversy has become a parable of exhortation, a word to the church. All the lost are not outside the church! In its concern for order and discipline, the church needs this reminder, lest its concern for order become legalism instead of love.

Matthew's change of setting makes for a change in detail. In Luke, the parable simply says that the shepherd has "lost one of them."

In Matthew, that lost one "has gone astray." In Luke the stress is on the shepherd's joy in finding, while in Matthew the stress is on his persistent search. However, both end with the joy of finding. Matthew's parable concludes that "it is not the will of my Father who is in heaven that one of these little ones [one of these least] should perish."

This is very different from the way in which The Gospel of Thomas interprets the shepherd's motive. There the shepherd seeks the lost sheep because it is the largest in the flock. But in Matthew, as in Luke, the shepherd seeks the least of the flock simply because it belongs to him. The shepherd cannot be content with a broken flock. Neither can God.

THE PARABLE TODAY

We must not blur the differences between Matthew and Luke. Both have relevance for today. Luke reminds us that the parable has a word for the world. Today the murmuring of the pharisees might not come from without the church but from within the church —it might be a complaint about the church's involvement with the world. The church must be ready to meet any criticism that would try to set limits for Christ's activity in the world. The Lucan form of the parable points us to the boundless love of God for the world. It reminds us why Christ must be there. It challenges us to be there.

Has Matthew, then, misunderstood the parable? Surely not. Matthew reminds us that we have not sufficiently heard the word if we think it is only addressed to those outside the community of faith. "Let *us* hear the word of God." Jesus' parable speaks not only to the understanding of the church's mission to the world. It speaks also to the church's understanding of herself. Sometimes we talk so callously about "cleaning up the roll" of the church membership. We talk so easily about real and nominal church members. In his *Church Dogmatics*, Karl Barth warns against the way we are prone to catalog people:

"The truth is that not merely some or many but all members of the Christian community stand under the sad possibility that they might not be real Christians, and yet that all and not merely some or many are called from death to life and therefore to the active life of service."

Bishop Gore once said that "love is the capacity to read statistics with compassion."

But Matthew's parable speaks of more than compassion. It speaks of a persistent search that leads to restoration and to the joy of finding. It speaks of the will of God, "not wishing that any should perish, but that all should reach repentance" (II Peter 3: 9).

The parable has its cutting edge in Luke's version and in Matthew's. We should allow the parable to speak to us in its distinctive way. If we do, we will discover what the writer to the Hebrews discovered about the way of God's word. "For the word of God is living and active, sharper than any two-edged sword, piercing to the division of soul and spirit, of joints and marrow, and discerning the thoughts and intentions of the heart. And before him no creature is hidden, but all are open and laid bare to the eyes of him with whom we have to do." (Heb. 4: 12-13.)

Luke's missionary situation remains today. Not only in the past but in the present Jesus sees the throngs and he has compassion for them "because they were like sheep without a shepherd" (Mark 6: 34). But Matthew's ecclesiastical situation also remains. As The First Letter of Peter puts it: "I exhort the elders among you, as a fellow elder. . . . *Tend the flock of God* that is your charge" (I Peter 5: 1-2).

Whether in the world or in the church, this parable of Jesus' points us to God's seeking love. We must not allegorize the parable. We need not allegorize it. The Lord who spoke this parable and who speaks it still is the One who elsewhere says, "I am the good shepherd; I know my own and my own know me . . ." (John 10: 14).

5

He Completes What He Has Begun

"We know that in everything God works for good with those who love him, who are called according to his purpose. For those whom he foreknew he also predestined to be conformed to the image of his Son, in order that he might be the first-born among many brethren. And those whom he predestined he also called; and those whom he called he also justified; and those whom he justified he also glorified." (Rom. 8: 28-30.)

THIS passage is often remembered and quoted only for its opening words as these are known in the King James Version:

"And we know that all things work together for good."

When these words are separated from their context they become a vague maxim, a curious combination of resignation and hope. Whatever must be must be—and somehow it will turn out all right in the end! We can almost hear Doris Day singing the popular tune of yesterday:

"Que será será—Whatever will be will be"!

But, if we are going to listen to Paul, we must not tear these words from their context. The apostle is not offering his readers a general proverb to accept life as it is. He is not expressing a pious wish that everything will turn out all right in the end. When we place these words in their context we discover that they are Paul's confession of faith. They are packed with his theology. They summarize his understanding of the gospel.

WHAT ROMANS IS ALL ABOUT

Before examining the passage in detail, we need to place it in Paul's letter. What does Paul have to say in this letter? We can trace his thought quickly.

Paul calls himself "a servant of Jesus Christ, called to be an apostle, set apart for the gospel of God" (ch. 1:1). He writes to expound "the gospel concerning his Son ... Jesus Christ our Lord" (vs. 3-4). He addresses those "who are called to belong to Jesus Christ ... called to be saints" (vs. 6-7). From beginning to end the letter is concerned with the gospel as "the power of God for salvation to every one who has faith" (v. 16).

This faith is not something that we can create. Paul follows the theme of the letter (ch. 1: 16-17) with a ruthless portrayal of the human predicament, a hopeless tragedy of sin and failure that stands under the wrath of God. (Chs. 1: 18 to 3: 20.) All things have *not* been working together for good. Rather, all men "have sinned and fall short of the glory of God" (ch. 3: 23).

But God can do what man cannot do. With ch. 3: 21 we turn to the good news of God. Men have failed, but God has not failed. God has given his righteousness to those who were not righteous. This is the gospel's answer to the hopelessness and futility that have marked the human situation. God's righteousness is not an impossible command but a saving deliverance, given to men in Jesus Christ. In the next chapter Paul turns to Abraham, for "Abraham believed God, and it was reckoned to him as righteousness" (ch. 4: 3). God's righteousness is given without merit and without limit. In ch. 5, human history is painted in even larger strokes as the history of Adam and the history of Christ. Christ has brought a new humanity into existence, bringing deliverance from sin and death (ch. 6) and deliverance from the condemnation of the law (ch. 7). That chapter closes with the joyful cry: "Thanks be to God through Jesus Christ our Lord!" (ch. 7: 25).

In ch. 8 all this is gathered together in a description of the new life in the Spirit. "But ye are not in the flesh, but in the Spirit, if so be that the Spirit of God dwell in you." (V. 9, KJV.) When we live in the Spirit, when we live "in Christ," we can live as the children of God who call him "Father" (v. 16). And if we are children, Paul goes on, then we are heirs of God and fellow heirs with Christ. But this is not a "cheap grace." To be a fellow heir with Christ means to become like him—"provided we suffer with him in order that we may also be glorified with him" (ch. 8: 17).

This brings us to the passage (ch. 8: 18-30) of which our text is a part. Paul compares the present with the future. "I consider that the sufferings of this present time are not worth comparing with the glory that is to be revealed to us." (V. 18.) Paul recognizes that the Christian lives in this world as well as in the Spirit. This life involves suffering (and Paul means suffering for the sake of Christ). But the Christian is not alone in his trial. Indeed, the whole creation is groaning as though in childbirth, waiting for the completion of God's purpose (v. 21). We know all too well our own helplessness, even our helplessness in prayer as we "groan inwardly" and wait for the full redemption (v. 28). But we are not left alone, for even the Spirit "groans" (KJV) and "intercedes for us with groanings which cannot be uttered" (v. 26, KJV). That is good news: "because the Spirit intercedes *for the saints according to the will of God*" (v. 27).

The Spirit intercedes for the saints, and the saints are those whom God has called (ch. 1: 7). Now follows the passage we shall examine in detail in which Paul summarizes with awe and wonder this will of God which reaches from eternity and reaches to eternity.

"What then shall we say to this?" (Ch. 8: 31.) Why, if God is for us, who can be against us? And so the chapter closes with the joyous affirmation that nothing in all creation "will be able to separate us from the love of God in Christ Jesus our Lord" (v. 39).

But the apostle is not yet finished with "the will of God." If he has earlier said that the gospel is for the Jew first and also for the Greek (ch. 1: 16), this will of God must ultimately embrace both Jew and Gentile so that "all Israel will be saved" (ch. 11: 26). This is the concern of chs. 9 to 11. When Paul reaches this conviction that "all Israel will be saved," he does so with the same jubilant wonder with which ch. 8 closes. "O the depth of the riches and wisdom and knowledge of God! . . . For from him and through him and to him are all things. To him be glory for ever. Amen." (Ch. 11: 33, 36.)

With the sure mercies of God as a basis, the remainder of the letter deals with the ethical implications of the gospel.

Now, let us look more closely at the particular text.

FAITH FOR LIVING

"We know that in everything God works for good with those who love him." Who is "we"? Clearly, those who have been "called to belong to Jesus Christ" (ch. 1: 1, 6).

We know that *in everything*, in *all things*, God works for good with those who love him. What does Paul mean when he says "all things"? Clearly, he means especially those sufferings which Christians must endure. Paul is not philosophizing about things-in-general. He is thinking of "the sufferings of this present time" (ch. 8: 18). Paul's theme here is faith joined with hope—for the living of these days. Paul does not pretend that God's purpose is always self-evident, but he knows that faith and hope belong together.

Our passage is a Christian confession of faith—for the living of these days. Having seen what kind of passage it is, we must examine it in more detail.

UNCERTAINTIES IN TRANSLATION

First of all, we need to compare the translation of the passage as we find it in the Revised Standard Version with that of the King James Version and with the marginal comment of the Revised Standard. Notice the difference: The King James Version (and the RSV margin) reads: "And we know that all things work together for good to them that love God." The RSV itself reads: "We know that in everything God works for good with those who love him."

A good commentary will tell us why the translation is uncertain. It is not a matter of manuscripts but simply of grammar. In Greek, the neuter plural is spelled the same whether it is a subject or an object. A neuter plural noun takes a singular verb. In our text, the neuter plural noun ("all things") is followed by a singular verb ("works together with"). This *can* mean that Paul means "all things" as the subject of the verb that follows. That is the way in which the King James translators and the RSV margin read the passage. But in Greek the object often precedes the verb. In that case the RSV is correct in reading that "he" (God) works together for good all things (in everything). Some very early manuscripts made this reading explicit by including the word "God" a second time for emphasis: "We know that to those who love God, God works all things for good." Such an insertion shows that those early scribal editors believed that Paul meant "all things" to be the object and not the subject of the verb. This debate continues into some of the latest commentaries on the letter.

How shall we read it? Because Paul always thinks of the will of God in very personal terms, we may conclude that the RSV stresses what Paul intends to say. In all things, including those trials which we do not understand, God is at work for those who love him. In any case, whether we read the sentence as the KJV does or as the RSV does, we can agree that Paul intends us to understand the will of God in personal terms. He confesses his faith in the personal will of a personal God revealed in Jesus Christ. This is not a Stoic resignation that things will work out somehow.

SOME KEY WORDS IN PAUL'S VOCABULARY

When we have decided how we shall read the first verse, we have not completed our "translation." The more important translation involves our understanding of the key words in this passage.

A study of individual words is more important for our understanding of some passages of Scripture than it is for others. For example, we do not necessarily catch the mood of a poem by a dissection of its individual words. We might even lose the whole while analyzing the parts. But for a passage such as Rom. 8: 28-30 we very much need to examine each of the key words carefully. Few passages in the New Testament have a greater concentration of "loaded" words. Each word is packed with Paul's theology. With the help of a concordance, a Bible wordbook, and perhaps a volume on New Testament theology we can set ourselves to "translate" Paul's meaning.

We shall take the key words in the order in which they appear in the RSV.

1. "We know that **in everything** God works for good" (literally: "We know that God works *all things* for good").

The context has already shown us that "all things" find their immediate reference in the sufferings that mark the Christian's life in the world. This is no new concern, for already in ch. 5: 3-5, Paul had said: "More than that, we rejoice in our sufferings, knowing that suffering produces endurance, and endurance produces character, and character produces hope, and hope does not disappoint us, because God's love has been poured into our hearts."

But Paul's thought probably goes beyond this. He has said that everywhere and in everything God is working his purpose out. He has just said: "We know that the whole creation has been groaning in travail together until now" (ch. 8: 22). Paul does not limit God's purpose to the saving of individual persons; he looks for a redemption of the whole creation. A concordance will show us other examples of how "all things" are embraced in God's purpose. Here are a few:

"He who did not spare his own Son but gave him up for us all, will he not also give us *all things* with him?" (Rom. 8: 32.)

"For from him and through him and to him are *all things*." (Rom. 11: 36.)

"For *all things* are yours, . . . all are yours; and you are Christ's; and Christ is God's." (I Cor. 3: 21-23.)

"Yet for us there is one God, the Father, from whom are *all things* and for whom we exist, and one Lord, Jesus Christ, through whom are *all things* and through whom we exist." (I Cor. 8: 6.)

"'For God has put *all things* in subjection under his feet' . . . that God may be everything to every one [all in all]." (I Cor. 15: 27-28.)
"[Christ] is before *all things*, and in him *all things* hold together." (Col. 1: 17.)

The letter to the Ephesians carries this theme even farther:

"For he has made known to us . . . the mystery of his will, according to his purpose which he set forth in Christ as a plan for the fulness of time, to unite *all things* in him, things in heaven and things on earth." (Eph. 1: 9-10.)

All things embrace the sufferings which Christians now experience, but it reaches farther. It embraces the whole of God's purpose.

2. "We know that in everything **God** works for good with those who love him."

In the eighteenth century, Deism was a popular philosophy which held that God was a "first cause" who set the universe running as a clockmaker sets a clock running. But now the clock runs by itself. We still meet practical deists, even in the church, who think of God as an absentee God who has virtually retired from the scene. But the God of Biblical faith is always "the living God." He is no first cause. He is active in all that happens—in storm and in stress, in mercy and in judgment, in the affairs of nations as well as in the order of nature. Jesus answered the "deists" of his day with the words: "My Father is working still, and I am working" (John 5: 17).

This was Paul's faith. And in our passage Paul says that God works with and through those who love him. God does not "go it alone." He includes us in his work. Paul expresses this in other places as well:

"For we are fellow workers for God; you are God's field, God's building." (I Cor. 3: 9.)

"Working together with him, then, we entreat you not to accept the grace of God in vain." (II Cor. 6: 1.)

3. "God works **for good** with those who love him." God's will and work can only be good. When Paul begins the last part of his letter, he does so with the reminder "that you may prove what is the will of God, what is good and acceptable and perfect" (ch. 12: 2). For Paul, this "good" includes God's activity in the secular realm, for the state authority is "God's servant for your good" (ch. 13: 4). Of course Paul is not alone in saying that God's will is good. Jewish rabbinic writers said this too: "Everything which the Almighty does, he does for good."

4. "God works for good with **those who love him.**" And who are they? They "are *called* according to his purpose." They are "called to belong to Jesus Christ" (ch. 1: 6), "called to be saints" (v. 7). They can love God because they are "God's beloved" (v. 7). Paul knows that God's love is prior to any response of love that men can offer. "But God shows his love for us in that while we were yet sinners Christ died for us." (Ch. 5: 8.)

All Christians are "called." God is a God who calls (ch. 1: 1, 6-7). Such language takes us back to the Old Testament conception of God calling Israel to be his people. In the New Testament this stress on calling is especially characteristic of Paul. And we need to see that except for Rom. 1: 1 and I Cor. 1: 1, Paul always uses "calling" in the plural. As Alan Richardson puts it: "Christians are corporately 'the called' and corporately 'the elect,' and they are these things . . . because they are one body in Christ, the Elect One." (*An Introduction to the Theology of the New Testament.*)

What is the basis of this calling? Paul goes on to tell us.

5. "Who are called **according to his purpose.**" What does Paul mean by God's purpose? In the following chapter he speaks of "God's purpose of election" (ch. 9: 11). In the later letters this note is even stronger:

"In him, according to the purpose of him who accomplishes all things according to the counsel of his will, we who first hoped in Christ have been destined and appointed to live for the praise of his glory." (Eph. 1: 11.)

"God, who saved us and called us with a holy calling, not in virtue of our works but in virtue of his own purpose and the grace which he gave us in Christ Jesus ages ago . . . ." (II Tim. 1: 8-9.)

Paul does not talk about a purpose of God in general. He confesses his faith in God's purpose in Christ.

6. "For those whom he **foreknew** he also **predestined** to be conformed to the image of his Son."

What does Paul mean by the foreknowledge of God? Does he

mean that God knows beforehand what is going to happen and then
accepts this as his purpose?

No. A concordance shows that the Bible never portrays God as
one who sits on the sidelines, seeing what is going to happen and
then accepting this as his will. The God of the Bible is always the
Lord. We should look up the way in which the Old Testament word
"to know" (Hebrew: *yada'*) and the way in which the New Testament word "to know" (Greek: *ginōskein*) are used. What would we
find?

In Genesis we read that Adam "*knew* his wife" (Gen. 4: 1). That
does not mean that Adam knew his wife was there! It refers to
sexual intercourse. The Old Testament uses this expression because
sexual intercourse is the most personal knowledge possible to a man
and a woman. It is knowledge with mutual commitment. The Old
Testament also uses this metaphor to speak of God's relationship
with Israel. God "knows" Israel because he has claimed Israel and
bound himself in faithfulness to her through a covenant.

> "You only have I known
>   of all the families of the earth."
>   (Amos 3: 2.)

> "I know Ephraim,
>   and Israel is not hid from me."
>   (Hos. 5: 3.)

It is no accident that Hosea follows this passage immediately
with a denunciation of Israel's sin. He accuses Israel of playing the
harlot against God.

From this it follows that when the Old Testament speaks of God's
foreknowing, it points to God's covenant relationship. That relationship is an eternal one. God's foreknowledge is God's predestination.

> "Before I formed you in the womb I knew you,
>   and before you were born I consecrated you;
>   I appoint you a prophet to the nations."
>   (Jer. 1: 5.)

Another personal expression of this foreknowledge of God is Ps. 139, which begins: "O Lord, thou hast searched me and known me!"

It is this foreknowing which Paul has in mind when he says that "God predestined whom he foreknew." The two words are really synonymous. This is not unique to Paul. Biblical faith never separated foreknowledge from predestination. At Pentecost, Peter said: "This Jesus, delivered up according to the *definite plan* and *foreknowledge* of God . . ." (Acts 2: 23). Notice that here the predestined purpose ("definite plan") and "foreknowledge" are in reverse order.

To say that God "knows" us from eternity is to say that God has "destined" us from eternity.

Let us remember what we have said earlier. This is a Christian confession of faith. It is not speculation about how many are "in" and how many are "out." When predestination is understood Biblically it is simply an adoring wonder and awe that God's grace has been given to those who do not merit his love. Too often predestination has been understood as something else—an arrogant boast that

> "We are God's chosen few,
>   All others will be damned;
> There is no place in heaven for you,
>   We can't have heaven crammed!"

Foreknowledge, predestination, election, calling—by whatever word we call God's grace—is simply a steadying certainty that our faith is in God and not in our own faith. Our faith may falter, but God is faithful. "But God's firm foundation stands, bearing this seal: 'The Lord knows those who are his.'" (II Tim. 2: 19.) Properly understood predestination is not a morbid or forbidding doctrine but a saving and joyful assurance that sings:

> "I sought the Lord, and afterward I knew
>   He moved my soul to seek Him, seeking me;
> It was not I that found, O Savior true;
>   No, I was found of Thee."

7. "For those whom he foreknew he also predestined **to be conformed to the image of his Son.**"

Those who are called to belong to Jesus Christ are called to be *like him.* Election is a matter of service, not of privilege.

For Paul, "to be like Christ" is both a present reality and a future hope. *How* are we to be like him? Paul often says that this must be a fellowship of his suffering:

"That I may know him and the power of his resurrection, and may share his sufferings, becoming *like him* in his death [Paul uses here the verbal form of the same word], that if possible I may attain the resurrection from the dead." (Phil. 3: 10-11.)

"Now I rejoice in my sufferings for your sake, and in my flesh I complete what is lacking in Christ's afflictions for the sake of his body, that is, the church." (Col. 1: 24.)

Again, writing of apostolic sufferings, he says: "Always carrying in the body the death of Jesus, so that the life of Jesus may also be manifested in our bodies" (II Cor. 4: 10). What is true of apostles is true of all who are called to belong to Christ: "For it has been granted to you that for the sake of Christ you should not only believe in him but also suffer for his sake" (Phil. 1: 29). Other New Testament writers point in the same direction (e.g., I Peter 2: 21).

We are reminded again that Paul had begun this section of Rom., ch. 8, with the words: "I consider that the sufferings of this present time are not worth comparing with the glory that is to be revealed to us" (v. 18). Paul did not have a martyr complex. Rather, this text is a reminder that election is for service and that grace is never a "cheap grace." After all, Jesus himself had said: "A disciple is not above his teacher, nor a servant above his master; it is enough for the disciple to be like his teacher, and the servant like his master" (Matt. 10: 24-25).

At the same time, to be "like Christ" is also our hope. Here the letter to the Philippians is a helpful commentary:

"But our commonwealth is in heaven, and from it we await a

Savior, the Lord Jesus Christ, who will change our lowly body to be *like* his glorious body, by the power which enables him even to subject all things to himself." (Phil. 3: 20-21.)

In this passage, the word translated "like" is exactly the same word translated "conformed to" in Rom. 8: 29.

8. "To be conformed to the **image of his Son**." Paul knows the word of Gen. 1: 26 that God created man in his own image. He has shown (Rom. 1: 18 to 3: 20) how all men fall short of the glory of God, exchanging the "glory of the immortal God for images resembling mortal man or birds or animals or reptiles" (ch. 1: 23). Only one man has perfectly expressed the image of God, Christ who is "the image of the invisible God, the first-born of all creation" (Col. 1: 15; see also II Cor. 4: 4). But Christians are a new creation. "Therefore, if any one is in Christ, he is a new creation; the old has passed away, behold, the new has come." (II Cor. 5: 17.) One day this new creation will be perfectly revealed. "Just as we have borne the image of the man of dust, we shall also bear the image of the man of heaven." (I Cor. 15: 49.)

Other New Testament writers express this same thought in different words. John writes: "See what love the Father has given us, that we should be called children of God. . . . Beloved, we are God's children now; it does not yet appear what we shall be, but we know that when he appears we shall be *like him,* for we shall see him as he is." (I John 3: 1-2.)

9. "That he might be the **first-born** among many brethren."
The firstborn is the "heir." In Col. 1: 15, Paul calls Christ not only the "image" but the "first-born."
What makes this good news is that this Christ who is the first-born and heir of all things has enabled his followers to become "joint-heirs" with him (Rom. 8: 17, KJV). For other New Testament expressions of this good news, read Heb. 2: 11, etc. Paul's hope is that Christ will be the firstborn among *many* brethren. How many? Paul's hope often reaches out to a day when "every knee should bow . . . and every tongue confess that Jesus Christ is Lord, to the glory of God the Father" (Phil. 2: 10-11).

10. "And those whom he predestined he also called; and those whom he called he also **justified.**"

While the noun "justification" occurs only in Rom. 4: 25 and 5: 18 (KJV), the verb "to justify" (to acquit, to count or make righteous) is continually on Paul's lips. A concordance will show that the verb appears 15 times in Romans and 8 times in Galatians. Outside the Pauline letters, the word appears only 11 other times in the New Testament. This means that here we are touching one of Paul's most characteristic and distinctive ways of describing the saving work of God. Our English translations somewhat obscure how dominant this theme is in Paul. We need to remember that the noun "righteousness" (*dikaiosunē*) has the same root as the verb we translate "to justify" (*dikaioun*).

Our sketch of the letter reminded us that the great theme is the righteousness of God. The human predicament is the situation of unrighteousness. ("None is righteous, no, not one." Rom. 3: 10.)

What is the "righteousness of God"? Paul means more than that righteousness is an attribute of God—that God is righteous. Were that all it would be no good news, for it would only mark more clearly the distance between a righteous God and unrighteous men. "But now the righteousness of God has been manifested apart from law." (Ch. 3: 21.) God's righteousness is *given* "through faith in Jesus Christ for all who believe" (v. 22). This *is* Paul's gospel. God's righteousness is revealed in the gospel (ch. 1: 16). "Therefore, since we are justified by faith, we have peace with God through our Lord Jesus Christ." (Ch. 5: 1.) Paul has laid hold of a truth that finds its best Old Testament expression in the prophet of the exile who can use "righteousness" and "salvation" as synonymous terms. (See Isa. 45: 8.) Paul gives a classic expression to the gospel tradition of Jesus who came "not to call the righteous but sinners to repentance."

When did God justify? Was it when Jesus died for sin and rose again? Paul can say this in Rom. 4: 25. But again, *when* did God justify? When a man turns to the Lord in faith? Paul never minimizes the importance of this act of faith. (See Rom. 6: 17-18.) *When* did God justify? Ultimately the question drives Paul back to the eternity of God's purpose. How deep are the roots of our Christian life? In our passage Paul suggests that God has loved us and justified us from eternity—and for eternity.

Accordingly, Paul does not give us a chronological order of saving events—as though God first foreknew and then predestined and then called and then justified. Instead, each of these great words describes the great redemption in Christ as from eternity and for eternity.

11. We come to the last of Paul's great words. "Those whom he justified he also **glorified**."

A Biblical confession of faith always keeps central God's glory. Paul has said that the human tragedy lay in men's exchanging the glory of the immortal God for images resembling mortal man. The tragedy can be summarized that "all have sinned and fall short of the glory of God" (ch. 3: 23). But Christians know that everything is for the glory of God. (See Rom. 11: 36; 16: 27; Phil. 2: 11; etc.) "That is why we utter the Amen through him, to the glory of God." (II Cor. 1: 20.) "We who first hoped in Christ have been destined and appointed to live for the praise of his glory." (Eph. 1: 12.) No wonder that the Shorter Catechism begins: "Man's chief end is to glorify God, and to enjoy him forever."

Let us not forget the latter—"and to enjoy him forever." The God of glory gives glory. Paul says, "We rejoice in our hope of sharing the glory of God." (Rom. 5: 2.) Immediately preceding our passage, he has said that we are to suffer with Christ as fellow heirs "in order that we may also be glorified with him" (ch. 8: 17).

Usually Paul speaks of "glorification" in the future tense. Occasionally he speaks of it as a present happening: "And we all, with unveiled face, beholding the glory of the Lord, *are being changed* into his likeness *from one degree of glory to another*" (II Cor. 3: 18). In our text, however, "glorified" is in the past tense: "Those whom he justified he also *glorified*." Why is this? Partly, it may be a matter of style. Since all the saving graces have been put in the past tense as rooted in the eternal purpose, so with "glorified." Yet it is more than a matter of style. Christian hoping and having belong together. What God will complete he has already begun. Elsewhere we find this same thought. In the Fourth Gospel, Jesus prays: "The glory which thou hast given me *I have given to them*" (John 17: 22).

The more we ponder these few verses the more we sense that

these great words are not for debate or dispute but for adoring wonder. Here Christian faith has reached a magnificent crescendo of certainty in God. "What then shall we say to this? If God is for us, who is against us?" (Rom. 8: 31.) This is the gospel according to Paul.

THE TEXT AND THEOLOGY

We are about to ask what the text means to us today. But before we do, let us review briefly how the text has been spoken to the church in the past. C. H. Dodd has rightly said that "for us men in Western Christendom there is probably no other single writing so deeply embedded in our heritage of thought" (The Moffatt Bible Commentary). The Letter of Paul to the Romans brought Augustine into the church. It largely shaped the thought of this great church leader and theologian who was to have such far-reaching influence on the church's later thought. Again, this letter was the great Scripture of the sixteenth-century Reformation. Through it Luther rediscovered the meaning of the gospel. (His lectures on Romans preceded by two years his manifesto which ignited the reformation movement.) John Calvin began his Biblical commentaries with a study of Romans. Once again, in our own century, Karl Barth's *Commentary on Romans* began a vigorous theological awakening. Time and again, this letter has been a word of renewal for Christian faith and life.

Accordingly, Paul's vocabulary of Christian faith comes to us through a particular heritage. We do not come to the text "out of the blue." We inevitably listen to Paul from the standpoint of some confessional heritage. For many of the readers of this book that heritage is "Calvinistic" or "Reformed."

So it is worth asking how the message of Rom. 8: 28-30 has been understood by this tradition. Although the Confession of 1967 was shaped more by II Cor. 5: 18-20, the Westminster Confession and the Shorter Catechism of the seventeenth century tried to define quite specifically Paul's vocabulary of faith which we find in Rom., ch. 8. For example, the Shorter Catechism asks such questions as: What is effectual calling? What is justification? What is adoption? If we study the history of theology, we will discover that Reformed theology has probed this passage very deeply. One result was to seek to interpret the "plan of salvation" as a logical sequence known as the *ordo salutis*, the order of salvation. Reformed theology tried to spell out how God's foreknowledge was related to his predestination. At its best, this older theology was not motivated by curiosity. Nor did it presume to do God's thinking for him. Reformed orthodoxy sought to take with full seriousness Paul's repeated claim. From beginning to end our salvation is God's doing and not our own.

For all their good intentions, the older Reformed theologians carried matters too far. In their attempt to understand the order of God's purpose, their reflections became highly theoretical and abstract—and unreal. For example, at the time that the Westminster Confession of Faith was written, Reformed theologians were engaged in heated debates on the order of salvation. Some said that God's election was *supralapsarian*—that is, that God decreed who the elect were quite apart from his decree of creation and the fact of the *lapsus*, or fall, of man. They wanted to say that creation is for redemption. Others maintained that God's predestination was *infralapsarian*—that is, that God predestined the elect out of the fallen creation. They wanted to say that the purpose of election is to save sinners.

But this whole attempt to spell out in some logical scheme the order of salvation is doomed to failure. The older theology could not find satisfying answers because it was asking the wrong questions. Here our Biblical studies can provide a needed corrective. Romans 8: 28-30 is not trying to spell out an order of salvation in God's eternal purpose. Rather, the apostle piles word upon word in order to express with awe and wonder the mystery of God's saving love that has claimed us *from* eternity and *for* eternity. "O the depth of the riches and wisdom and knowledge of God! How unsearchable are his judgments and how inscrutable his ways! 'For who has known the mind of the Lord, or who has been his counselor?' . . . For from him and through him and to him are all things. To him be glory for ever. Amen." (Rom. 11: 33-36.) In our worship and hymnody we know that this is where we must rest:

"Yea, through life, death, through sorrow and through sinning

He shall suffice me, for He hath sufficed;
Christ is the end, for Christ was the beginning,
Christ the beginning, for the end is Christ."

GOD IS FAITHFUL

This suggests what our passage means for Christian faith and life today. Speculations about an "order of salvation" do not help us. But the passage speaks to us where we are. It reminds us that God has loved us from eternity and for eternity in Jesus Christ. It reminds us that faith is *in God,* not in our own faltering faith. Emil Brunner has said: "Our life is 'superficial' without depth or meaning so long as it does not have its roots in eternity. Either it has eternal significance or it has no significance at all." (*Our Faith.*)

This has very practical implications. What happens to a Christian when he loses the joy of his salvation? What happens to a Christian when he feels all alone? What happens to a Christian when he is not sure of God? For it does happen. It may be some baffling and bewildering crisis that shatters his confidence in God. "My tears have been my food day and night, while men say to me continually, 'Where is your God?'" (Ps. 42: 3.) It may be some physical illness that leaves him prey to depression and desolation. Most of us have seen what a stroke or deteriorating mental health can do in the loss of spiritual confidence and of conscious communion. What are we to say in such a situation? Do we tell such a person that he must recapture somehow the feelings of a former day? Suppose he cannot? Does salvation depend on feelings—or on God? Isn't it nostalgic and unreal to try to recapture the feelings of yesterday? Is a familiar hymn right in even wishing it?

"Where is the blessedness I knew,
When first I saw the Lord?
Where is the soul-refreshing view
Of Jesus and His Word?"

But that is not the way in which we shall find "the soul-refreshing view."

How then? With or without a "soul-refreshing view," our Christian life is steadied by the reminder that it began and is sustained by God's eternal love. As Paul puts it again: "May the God of peace himself sanctify you wholly; and may your spirit and soul and body be kept sound and blameless at the coming of our Lord Jesus Christ. *He who calls you is faithful, and he will do it*" (I Thess. 5: 23-24). J. B. Phillips paraphrases the last sentence: "He who calls you is utterly faithful and he will finish what he has set out to do." This is Paul's constant theme: "Faithful is the God who called you to participate in his Son Jesus Christ our Lord" (I Cor. 1: 9, Moffatt).

Romans 8: 28-30 points us to how far this faithfulness of God reaches—from eternity to eternity. "Who shall separate us from the love of Christ?" (Rom. 8: 35.) Our passage has prepared us for the closing lines of the chapter:

"For I am sure that neither death, nor life, nor angels, nor principalities, nor things present, nor things to come, nor powers, nor height, nor depth, nor anything else in all creation, will be able to separate us from the love of God in Christ Jesus our Lord." (Rom. 8: 38-39.)

Postscript

BECAUSE *we often read too quickly and carelessly, it has seemed a useful discipline to introduce the task of interpretation by selecting a few very short passages for "time exposure."*

Our sampling of passages has shown that the problems in understanding vary with different kinds of passages. A more complete sampling would include at least one piece of poetry. Moreover, the interpreter will want and need to take a larger canvas at times— a whole chapter or even a whole book. Sometimes, too, he will want to explore a particular Biblical theme or topic as this appears in more than one Biblical writing.

We have tried to take into account the kinds of questions that a passage of Scripture raises, and to avoid the kinds of pitfalls to which we are all prone. (Chapter 1.)

Our conviction is that we learn by doing. We learn to interpret best not by reading books about interpretation (helpful as some of these are) but by interpreting—not by reading more books about the Bible but by reading the Bible itself. Our hope is that these samplings will convey something of the reward and excitement that come in Biblical study.

Let no one think that this is a task for experts. It is the task of every Christian who takes his Bible seriously. Particular methods of study will vary with the passages and with the persons who are doing the interpreting. But every method must help us to stand "at the point of viewing" if we are to find relevance and reality in "the point of view."

We are not left to ourselves in this task, because the Bible is the book of the church. We gratefully utilize every help that our fellow interpreters in the community of faith, past and present, have labored to provide.

We are not left to ourselves in this task, because we have the promise of God's Spirit. Jesus said, "But the Counselor, the Holy Spirit, whom the Father will send in my name, he will teach you all things, and bring to your remembrance all that I have said to you." (John 14: 26.)

A Bibliography of
Bible Study Aids

A Bibliography of
Bible Study Aids

(All the books listed below were in print at the date on which this bibliography was written. They may not be available for purchase at a later time. Most of the reference volumes, however, can be obtained from any public library.)

BIBLE ATLASES

Rand McNally Bible Atlas, by Emil G. Kraeling. Rand McNally & Company, 1956. A large volume, this Bible atlas contains extensive text material. The overall Biblical narrative is retold with special attention to historical and geographical items of importance. Maps, photos, and diagrams are plentiful and attractively reproduced.

The Westminster Historical Atlas to the Bible, ed. by George Ernest Wright and Floyd V. Filson. The Westminster Press, rev. ed., 1956. This is perhaps the best-known and most widely used atlas. The dimensions are 10″ x 14″ making possible large-scale map reproduction. This is a *historical* atlas. The authors provide extensive treatment of Israel's history and the history of the early Christian church. There are useful chronologies of ancient history, and the various advances in modern archaeology are described by the authors.

INTRODUCTIONS AND GENERAL WORKS

The Bible in Dialogue with Modern Man, by Peter W. Macky. Word Books, 1970. This introduction to the Bible for lay people is intended to help them hear through Scripture what the Spirit is saying to the churches today. It discusses the canon; the historical, literary, and theological nature of the Bible; and modern trends in Biblical scholarship, including a critical appraisal of Bultmann and the theology of hope. "A book to be read with profit by any intelligent person"—Dr. James I. McCord, president, Princeton Theological Seminary. 219 pages.

Song of the Vineyard: A Theological Introduction to the Old Testament, by B. Davie Napier. Harper & Row, 1962. This illustrated volume seeks to provide Christian lay persons with the knowledge that is essential to an understanding of the meaning of the Old Testament in the life and faith of Israel. It surveys the entire Old Testament text as a story "given form, coherence, and meaning by the life and purpose and power of God." 385 pages.

Introducing New Testament Theology, by Archibald M. Hunter. The Westminster Press, 1957. The opening chapters of this book deal with the "fact of Christ," his teaching of the Kingdom and his death and resurrection. Succeeding chapters focus on some of the "interpreters" of the fact of Christ, among them Paul, Peter, John. 160 pages.

The Bible in the Church: A Short History of Interpretation, by Robert M. Grant. The Macmillan Company, 1954. Written for the general reader, this short work traces the different ways the church has interpreted Scripture over the centuries. The concluding chapters take up modern developments in Biblical interpretation.

The Enduring Message of the Bible, by L. Harold DeWolf. John Knox Press, 1965. A straightforward statement of the Bible's answers to universal human issues: Where did we come from? Where are we going? How do we get there? 128 pages.

Our English Bible in the Making: The Word of Life in Living Language, by Herbert Gordon May. The Westminster Press, rev. ed.,

1965. The history of translations of the Bible into English is traced and the variations in different translations illustrated and explained.

Understanding the Bible, by Fred J. Denbeaux. (Layman's Theological Library.) The Westminster Press, 1958. This is a highly readable, fast-paced, and provocative invitation to the serious study of the Bible. 96 pages.

Mastering New Testament Facts, Books 1, 2, 3, and 4, by Madeline H. Beck and Lamar Williamson, Jr. John Knox Press, 1973. A self-study guide to the New Testament designed to help the student learn the content and structure of the New Testament in the shortest possible time. Concepts are reinforced through the use of line drawings, programmed reading, and tests. The four books are *Introduction and Synoptic Gospels, John and Acts, The Pauline Letters,* and *General Letters and Revelation.*

The Mighty Act of God, by A. B. Rhodes. CLC Press, 1964. This survey of the entire Bible stresses its essential unity and historical sweep. It comments on especially important passages as well as on major Biblical themes. 448 pages.

COMMENTARIES

The Layman's Bible Commentary, ed. by Balmer H. Kelly. John Knox Press, 1959–64. 25 vols. These volumes are written by Biblical scholars. The language is nontechnical. Volume 1 in the series is titled *Introduction to the Bible.* It contains five sections with the titles: "What Is the Bible?" "The History of the People of God," "The Message of the Bible," "How We Got the Bible," and "How to Study the Bible." Volume 1 is especially valuable to the beginning student of the Bible. Volumes 2 to 25 provide commentary on each of the books of the Bible.

The Interpreter's Bible: The Holy Scriptures in the King James and Revised Standard Versions. Editorial Board: George Arthur Buttrick, commentary editor, and others. Abingdon Press, 1951–1957. 12 vols. A standard reference work for pastors and laymen. These volumes contain exegesis of the text as well as exposition of its meaning for today. k.j.v. and r.s.v. translations of the Scripture are printed in parallel columns along with the exegesis and exposition. Especially useful for the lay student are the general articles on the Old Testament in volume 1 and on the New Testament in volume 7.

Interpreter's One-Volume Commentary on the Bible, edited by Charles M. Laymon. Abingdon Press, 1971. Not a brief summary of the 12-volume set, this is a new and highly useful commentary written by very competent authors.

The Cambridge Bible Commentary on the New English Bible. These volumes, ordinarily of about 160–196 pages each, are still appearing, though the New Testament section is now complete. Eventually there will be introductory volumes to each Testament, including a book for each of maps and pictures, plus a volume on each Bible book (or 2–3 short books). The text of the n.e.b. is printed along with the commentary. While this series reflects the best scholarship, it is definitely planned for students and lay people.

Concordances

Nelson's Complete Concordance of the Revised Standard Version Bible, ed. by John W. Ellison. Thomas Nelson & Sons, 1957. This concordance was compiled with the use of Univac I at the offices of Remington Rand, Inc. It does not indicate the Hebrew and Greek words that the r.s.v. translates. It is a very large volume. As in all concordances, the words are arranged alphabeticaly with the numbered Biblical reference. Each word is placed in the short phrase in which it occurs in the English text.

The Oxford Concise Concordance to the Revised Standard Version of the Holy Bible, comp. by Bruce M. Metzger and Isobel M. Metzger. Oxford University Press, 1962. A short concordance on the r.s.v. for the general reader.

Young's Analytical Concordance to the Bible. 22nd American edition, rev. by William B. Stevenson, with new supplement by William F. Albright. Funk & Wagnalls Company, 1955. This is a concordance on the words of the King James Version of the Bible. It includes the Hebrew or Greek words that are translated by the English word. Difficult texts and variant readings are indicated. A Lexicon-Index in the back of the concordance makes it possible to use this concordance, even though one is studying the R.S.V. text of the Bible. There are 1090 pages of word listings.

DICTIONARIES AND WORD BOOKS

The Interpreter's Dictionary of the Bible. Editorial Board: George Arthur Buttrick, dictionary editor, and others. Abingdon Press, 1962. 4 vols. An illustrated encyclopedia of the Bible containing detailed articles on the important names and terms of the Bible. These four volumes are perhaps the best single source of Biblical information for the general reader of the Bible today.

The New Westminster Dictionary of the Bible, edited by Henry S. Gehman. Westminster Press, 1970. This newly revised one-volume dictionary is quite useful to lay people.

Fifty Key Words: The Bible, by Julian Charley. John Knox Press, 1971. A quick-reference book with short, readable definitions of such terms as Body, Covenant, Devil, Faith, Flesh, Gospel, Hope, Law, Love, Miracle, Predestination, Saint, Servant, Soul, Wrath. 69 pages.

Probing the New Testament, by A. M. Hunter. John Knox Press, 1972. A delightful wordbook that covers 64 key New Testament ideas that strike Dr. Hunter's fancy—from a single word like "charisma" to a phrase like "a thorn in the flesh" to a chapter like Acts 27 to a whole book like Jude. 156 pages.

A Theological Word Book of the Bible, ed. by Alan Richardson. The Macmillan Company, 1950. This widely used volume contains brief essays on various words of the Bible that have particular theological importance. The items are cross-referenced. 290 pages.

HISTORIES AND SURVEYS

A History of Israel, second edition, by John Bright. The Westminster Press, 1972. A thorough revision of what is generally considered to be the standard survey of the history of Israel from the times of the patriarchs to the end of the Old Testament period. 519 pages, plus 16 plates of historical maps.

A New Testament History: The Story of the Emerging Church, by Floyd V. Filson. The Westminster Press, 1964. A highly useful volume containing historical background material on the New Testament period. This book deals with the career of Jesus and the rise of early Christianity, viewed against the background of New Testament times. 435 pages plus 16 plates of historical maps.

A Thousand Years and a Day: Our Time in the Old Testament, by Claus Westermann, tr. by Stanley Rudman. Fortress Press, 1962. A highly useful survey of the Old Testament written in nontechnical language. *The Day of His Coming: The Man in the Gospels,* by Gerhard Gloege, tr. by Stanley Rudman (Fortress Press, 1963) is a companion volume that deals with Jesus' world, his claims about himself, and the force of those claims in the world today. The "thousand years" of Israel's history culminates in the "day" of Christ and his church.

MODERN VERSIONS AND EDITIONS

The Holy Bible. Revised Standard Version. The R.S.V. is not a fresh translation of the Scriptures into modern speech but a revision of the "authorized" or King James Version. A second edition of the New Testament was published early in 1973 to incorporate some comparatively minor modifications of the text to make it more accurate and more intelligible.

The Whole New English Bible. Oxford University Press and Cambridge University Press, 1961. A fresh translation of the Scriptures into modern speech carried out in the British Isles under joint church auspices.

The New Testament in Modern English, ed. by J. B. Phillips. The Macmillan Company, 1958. The first installment of this translation to appear was the Epistles. It was published under the title, *Letters to Young Churches,* and was very popular. Later, the Gospels and Revelation were translated and the entire New Testament was published in a single volume.

Today's English Version: Good News for Modern Man, American Bible Society, 1966. This simple, clear translation of the New Testament has achieved immense popularity. A similar translation of the Old Testament is in process.

The Oxford Annotated Bible: The Revised Standard Version, ed. by Herbert G. May and Bruce M. Metzger. Oxford University Press, 1962. This edition of the R.S.V. provides scholarly notes on the text and numerous references. The notes appear at the foot of the page and do not intrude on the Biblical text itself. In addition to the notes there are color maps and chronological tables. Another valuable feature of this edition is two articles, "How to Read the Bible with Understanding" and "Survey of the Geography, History, and Archaeology of Bible Lands."

QUESTIONS

THE QUESTIONS BELOW can aid your study in two ways. The first few questions in each chapter section may serve as a handy means for reviewing the contents of the book itself. The questions in italics are offered as examples—but examples only—of types of questions that might be fruitful for group discussion. The questions you actually use in group discussion should arise out of your particular inquiry, and should be stated in terms that are most meaningful to members of the group. The booklet *Guided Group Study* contains further suggestions on how to plan and carry out book-related study.

(**Chapter 1**) What does the story of Philip and the eunuch (Acts, ch. 8) suggest to us about how to understand the Bible? Can you define "exegesis"? "hermeneutics"? What are some of the reasons for misinterpretation of Scripture? Does one have to understand the whole Bible before he can accurately interpret a single passage? What are some of the questions the interpreter should raise as he studies a text? Do particular interpretations of Scripture hold true for all time? If not, does the Biblical word change from generation to generation? *Every interpreter brings his own perspective to the study of Scripture. Can you identify your own biases as an interpreter? If someone claimed to have discovered a "new" truth in his study of the Bible, how would you determine whether it was really fresh light on God's word or just someone's bright idea?*

(**Chapter 2**) Which came first in Old Testament faith, confession of God as Creator or confession of God as Redeemer? Of what larger segment of the Old Testament is Genesis a part? What are some of the similarities and differences in the two accounts of Creation? How do scholars account for these differences? Is the basic message of the two accounts the same or different? How do problems in translation of a text affect our theological understanding of Gen. 1: 1-2? How might our theology influence our translation of the same text? How does the Genesis narrative of Creation differ from the Babylonian epic? *What significance does the Genesis account of Creation have for the modern scientific age?*

(**Chapter 3**) Describe in your own words the historical circumstances that form the background for Isa. 7: 10-17. What in brief is the prophet's message in this time of crisis in Judah? Explain in your own words the problem of translation that arises in Isa. 7: 14 ("young woman" or "virgin"). Why has this text created so much controversy? What is at issue in this text in relation to our understanding of the role of the prophet? What is a "sign"? What does the sign of Immanuel mean to us? How did the New Testament writers use the Old Testament? What stands out in

Matthew's use of Old Testament passages? What meaning did Matthew apply to Isa. 7: 14? Was he making proper use of the Old Testament in doing so? *What does the doctrine of the virgin birth mean to you? How would you go about interpreting your view of this doctrine to a sixth-grader? Where does God meet us? What sign has he given to us in our world with all its problems and unrest? Can the meaning of this sign be shared? Does it affect our action as Christians? If so, in what ways?*

(**Chapter 4**) Can you define the word "parable"? (Indicate what a parable is not, as well as what it is.) Why did Jesus teach in parables? Were the parables intended as "illustrations"? If so, do they make difficult meanings more clear? What are some things to keep in mind in interpreting a parable? Can you put your finger on the difference between Luke's version and Matthew's version of the parable of the lost sheep? *Does the church today persistently seek the lost one? How can the attempt to restore one who has gone astray be carried out so that he is not repelled instead of being restored to the church's fellowship? Who are lost? Who are "in the fold"?*

(**Chapter 5**) What is Paul's estimate of the human situation? What has God done about man's predicament? What is the nature of the day-to-day existence of those whom God has called in Christ? Does the gospel save us from suffering? State in your own words the difficulties in translation that arise in Rom. 8: 28-30. Do these difficulties greatly affect its interpretation? Lay this book aside and go through the text of Rom. 8: 28-30, explaining in your own words individual words and phrases. What is the main theological problem that has arisen in relation to this text? Why is the effort to spell out an "order of salvation" unwise? *What are some of the practical implications of Rom. 8: 28-30 for the Christian today? Does the knowledge of God's eternal purpose and our share in it serve as a corrective for our changes in mood from day to day? Or is the idea of God's eternal purpose in Jesus Christ too abstract to be of practical value in everyday life?*

Other Titles in the
BIBLE STUDIES FOR MODERN MAN
Series

The Covenants in Faith and History   *Stephen Szikszai*

A chain of covenants binds together the history of the people of God in the Old and New Testaments. In this book Stephen Szikszai describes six crucial covenant-making events recorded in the Bible. The first is the covenant with Moses at Mt. Sinai. Significant occasions of covenant renewal took place in the times of Joshua, David, Josiah, and Ezra. The series of covenants came to a climax in the New Covenant of Jesus Christ and the formation of God's new people, the church. Covenant renewal continues in the church through worship and sacrament. The task of the people of God in the Bible and in today's church is the healing of mankind.

The Word in Action:
The Acts of the Apostles for Our Time   *Ross Mackenzie*

As we reach out to a world of revolution, violence, dilemmas, and hopes, how is the gospel of Jesus Christ a "word in action" for our day? Ross Mackenzie answers this question by exploring incidents from the Book of Acts that shed light on corresponding issues today. He focuses on episodes that played a decisive role in shaping the young church. Each chapter closes with several quotations from contemporary sources that serve as two-way probes into Acts and the current scene. The result is a book that gathers insights from Acts to help us face the challenges of our world in the grace of Christ and the power of the Spirit. An invaluable resource for the study of evangelism.

Leader's Guide to   *Mac N. and*
Bible Studies for Modern Man   *Anne Shaw Turnage*

These session-by-session helps are for those who lead adults or older youth in the study of the three books in the Bible Studies for Modern Man series.